Artificial Intelligence

OTHER TITLES IN THE TECHNOLOGY 360 SERIES:

TECHNOLOGY 360

Artificial Intelligence

Q. L. Pearce

LUCENT BOOKS
A part of Gale, Cengage Learning

GALE
CENGAGE Learning™

Detroit • New York • San Francisco • New Haven, Conn • Waterville, Maine • London

LIBRARY OF CONGRESS CATALOGING-IN-PUBLICATION DATA

Pearce, Q. L. (Querida Lee)
    Artificial intelligence / by Q. L. Pearce.
        p. cm. — (Technology 360)
    Includes bibliographical references and index.
    ISBN 978-1-4205-0384-5 (hardcover)
    1. Artificial intelligence. 2. Conscious automata. 3. Robots—Control. I. Title.
    Q335.P3793 2011
    006.3—dc22

                                                                2011006362

Lucent Books
27500 Drake Rd
Farmington Hills MI 48331

ISBN-13: 978-1-4205-0384-5
ISBN-10: 1-4205-0384-7

Printed in the United States of America
1 2 3 4 5 6 7 15 14 13 12 11
Printed by Bang Printing, Brainerd, MN, 1st Ptg., 06/2011

CONTENTS

FOREWORD

"As we go forward, I hope we're going to continue to use technology to make really big differences in how people live and work."
—Sergey Brin, co-founder of Google

The past few decades have seen some amazing advances in technology. Many of these changes have had a direct and measureable impact on the way people live, work, and play. Communication tools, such as cell phones, satellites, and the Internet, allow people to keep in constant contact across longer distances and from the most remote places. In fields related to medicine, existing technologies—digital imaging devices, robotics and lasers, for example—are being used to redefine surgical procedures and diagnostic techniques. As technology has become more complex, however, so have the related ethical, legal, and safety issues.

Psychologist B.F. Skinner once noted that "the real problem is not whether machines think but whether men do." Recent advances in technology have, in many cases, drastically changed the way people view the world around them. They can have a conversation with someone across the globe at lightening speed, access a huge universe of information with the click of a key, or become an avatar in a virtual world of their own making. While advances like these have been viewed as a great boon in some quarters, they have also opened the door to questions about whether or not the speed of technological advancement has come at an unspoken price. A closer examination of the evolution and use of these devices provides a deeper understanding of the social, cultural and ethical implications that they may hold for our future.

Technology 360 not only explores how evolving technologies work, but also examines the short- and long-term impact of their use on society as a whole. Each volume in Technology 360 focuses on a particular invention, device or family of similar devices, exploring how the device was developed; how it works; its impact on society; and possible future uses. Volumes also contain a timeline specific to each topic, a glossary of technical terms used in the text, and a subject index. Sidebars, photos and detailed illustrations, tables, charts and graphs help further illuminate the text.

Titles in this series emphasize inventions and devices familiar to most readers, such as robotics, digital cameras, iPods, and video games. Not only will users get an easy-to-understand, "nuts and bolts" overview of these inventions, they will also learn just how much these devices have evolved. For example, in 1973 a Motorola cell phone weighed about 2 pounds (.907 kg) and cost $4000.00—today, cell phones weigh only a few ounces and are inexpensive enough for every member of the family to have one. Lasers—long a staple of the industrial world—have become highly effective surgical tools, capable of reshaping the cornea of the eye and cleaning clogged arteries. Early video games were played on large machines in arcades; now, many families play games on sophisticated home systems that allow for multiple players and cross-location networking.

IMPORTANT DATES

1948/1949
Grey Walter builds autonomous robots, Elsie and Elmer based on the idea that a small number of brain cells could give rise to complex behaviors.

1950
Alan Turing published Computing Machinery and Intelligence and introduced the Turing Test as a way of determining intelligent behavior by a computer.

1956
John McCarthy coined the term *artificial intelligence* as the topic of the Dartmouth Conference, the first conference devoted to the subject.

1952
Arthur Samuel wrote the first checkers program for a computer

1950

1960

1834
Charles Babbage developed plans for the Analytical Engine.

1963
Edward A. Feigenbaum & Julian Feldman published Computers and Thought, the first collection of articles about artificial intelligence.

1967
Dendral program becomes the first successful knowledge-based program for scientific reasoning.

in the Development of Artificial Intelligence

1969
Shakey the robot is introduced and the First International Joint Conference on Artificial Intelligence is held in Washington, D.C.

2006
The Dartmouth Artificial Intelligence Conference: The Next 50 Years takes place July 14–16.

2005
Honda debuts the autonomous robot ASIMO. In the same year the Blue Brain project begins work on creating a slice of a simulated rat brain.

1987
Marvin Minsky publishes The Society of Mind, a theoretical description of the mind as a collection of cooperating agents.

1997
The Deep Blue chess program beats world chess champion, Garry Kasparov in a six-game match. In the same year, the Pathfinder spacecraft touches down on Mars and releases the Sojourner robot rover.

1998 Cynthia Breazeal at MIT starts work on the Kismet robot, which can mimic the emotional range of a baby.

1980

2000

1979
The Stanford Cart, built by Hans Moravec, becomes the first computer-controlled, autonomous vehicle.

2010
In November, Microsoft releases the Kinect for Xbox 360 – a hands-free video game system that utilizes artificial intelligence elements such as motion sensors and voice recognition.

Artificial Intelligence: Myth to Reality

Humans have been designing forms of artificial intelligence (AI) for more than two thousand years. An ancient Greek myth tells of Talos, a giant warrior that was a machine made of bronze. It guarded the island of Crete from invaders. According to the myth, Talos was created by Hephaestus (hay-FESS-tus), the god of fire and metalworking. Hephaestus is credited with creating many magical objects designed to serve their owners, such as the winged helmet and winged sandals of the Greek god Hermes that enabled him to fly. Hephaestus is also said to have built an array of smart machines that resembled humans and animals, including two fire-breathing horses, a pair of silver and gold watchdogs, and two golden maidens who took care of the household for Hephaestus. According to myth, he also assembled a troop of mechanical men to help him in his workshop. In his great poem, *The Iliad*, the Greek historian Homer (eighth century B.C.) refers to artificial servants who help Hephaestus forge new armor for the hero Achilles.

Although the mechanical beings of Hephaestus are myth, the Greeks did build many figures called automatons. *Automaton* is from a Greek word that means acting of one's own will. They were machines with moving parts. The moveable figures were powered by wind, water, and steam. They were used mainly as toys or for entertainment.

In the twelfth century, Muslim engineer al-Jazari (1136–1206) created a musical robot band powered by water. As the band played a tune, the human-like figures displayed a wide range of body actions and facial expressions. Even the famed Renaissance artist Leonardo da Vinci (1452–1519) designed a mechanical human. Modern engineers agree that if made, it would have been able to sit up, move its arms, and turn its head.

Hephaestus, the Greek god of blacksmiths and metal workers, is said to have created Talos, a giant warrior made of bronze who guarded the island of Crete.

By the late 1800s, scientists were building machines that did more than entertain. A few could carry out simple mathematical calculations and create mathematical tables. Despite these advances, scientists still had not created machines that could move independently or think for themselves. These types of machines did exist, however, in science-fiction novels and plays. In 1920 a Czech playwright named Karel Capek wrote a play called *Rossum's Universal Robots*. Capek introduced the term *robota*, or robots, to describe the intelligent machines portrayed in his story. The main character was a professor who created artificial humans to do tasks that most people did not want to do. Over time the robots were used for unethical purposes, such as fighting in wars as soldiers. When a scientist developed a way to give them human emotions, the robots revolted against their human masters.

In modern times, AI, sometimes called machine intelligence, refers to the ability of a manufactured machine to mimic elements of human intelligence. When robots and computers became a reality in the twentieth century, the possibilities of artificial intelligence captured the imagination of the public. Films that included robots and

Droids R2-D2, left, and C-3PO, robots that exhibited many human qualities, were among the Star Wars *film series' most popular characters.*

supercomputers became popular. *The Day the Earth Stood Still* (1951) features a huge robot named Gort designed by aliens to enforce universal laws. The movie *Colossus: The Forbin Project* (1969) is about a supercomputer that takes over U.S. national defense systems. The robot stars of the 1970s *Star Wars* series, C-3PO and R2-D2, help save the universe. Although they are obviously made of metal and gears, the two display many human emotions, including fear, loyalty, and courage. AI is best depicted in the feature film *A.I. Artificial Intelligence* (2001) about a lifelike robot boy who wishes for nothing more than the love of his adoptive human mother.

In the twenty-first century, science fiction is quickly becoming fact. Scientists who are working to create intelligent machines have made tremendous strides in computer programming and robotic engineering. In modern society humans rely on AI in the form of computers, GPS (global positioning system), navigation systems, and a host of gadgets that perform tasks that make life easier, safer, and more interesting. Supercomputers do everything from controlling space vehicles as they explore other planets to creating spectacular special effects for blockbuster movies. Robotic devices labor in factories; are used by the military and law enforcement to perform dangerous tasks, such as disposing of explosives; and may even be found vacuuming the carpet in family homes. Computers allow many people to work from home. In the near future doctors may be able to perform certain medical procedures on patients located many miles away by using a combination of computer systems and robotics.

Still, the outlook for AI is not all rosy. There may be disadvantages. Some people are concerned that human workers in factory and service jobs might be replaced with robots. Others worry that humans may become too dependent on AI and lose important physical and mental skills. Some critics point out that even advanced machines can malfunction. Will advances in AI continue to benefit humanity? Will the creation of an intelligent machine put the human species in danger? Will the benefits of AI outweigh the risks? As of the beginning of the twenty-first century, the answers are unknown.

CHAPTER 1

The First Steps

The path to true artificial intelligence (AI), or machine intelligence, began with the development of the programmable computer, a machine that could manipulate data according to instructions, or programs, from a human operator. The first simple automatic calculating machines led to more complex ideas and the idea of creating a thinking machine slowly took shape.

Charles Babbage and Faster Calculations

Many people consider Charles Babbage (1792–1871), an English mathematician and inventor, to be the father of the computer. Babbage was a brilliant scientist. He belonged to the Royal Society, a scientific academy, in the United Kingdom and was a professor at Cambridge University in England from 1828 to 1839.

Babbage began his quest for a dependable automatic calculator in the early 1800s. At that time teams of young men and women, called computers, created mathematical tables. It was faster for people to look up an answer on a table than to calculate the answer themselves, so the tables the computers created were regularly used in math, science, the military, and many other fields. The captain of an oceangoing ship would use a table to determine the position of the craft at sea. Engineers used them to design bridges. Bankers and insurance brokers relied on mathematical tables when they estimated interest rates and fees.

The tables created by human computers were calculated, noted, copied, and typeset by hand, which meant that errors could be introduced at every step. Mistakes in certain tables were costly, and some led to terrible accidents, such as shipwrecks. Babbage's friend, astronomer Sir John Herschel said, "An undetected error in a logarithmic table is much like a sunken rock at sea yet undiscovered, upon which it is impossible to say what wrecks may have taken place."[1] Babbage thought that the possibility of human error was also increased by the fact that creating mathematical tables could be boring work. He wanted to develop a machine that would calculate tables faster and more reliably than human computers could.

English mathematician and inventor Charles Babbage drafted plans for automatic calculating machines that are considered early versions of the modern computer.

In 1822 Babbage began plans for a machine that he called the difference engine, which was something like a huge mechanical calculator. His idea was for a machine that could find the differences between rows of numbers and print out completed tables. Babbage designed the difference engine to be operated by a person turning a crank many times for each calculation. Information, in the form of rows of punched holes, would be fed to the machine on input cards. The holes in each card determined which levers would be activated and in what order. The levers corresponded to numbers on number wheels in the machine. The completed calculations would be delivered on cards.

When a section of the unfinished machine was complete, Babbage invited members of the Royal Astronomical Society to see a demonstration, and many were impressed. At first it

The Difference Engine No. 2

Charles Babbage drew up plans for the Difference Engine No. 2 between 1847 and 1849. He combined ideas from the first difference engine and the analytical engine to create a new, improved design. The machine had similar computing power to earlier models, but it had fewer parts and was much smaller. More than a century passed before it was actually built.

In 1985 Doron Swade, the curator of computing at the Science Museum in London, began a project to construct a working Difference Engine No. 2. Engineers finished the main part of the machine in 1991, using the original plans. It was built to honor Babbage's two hundredth birthday. The printing mechanism, which can be programmed for an output of one to three columns, was added in 2002 as the final component of the seventeen-year project. The completed machine has about eight thousand

parts. It is 7 feet (2.1m) high and 11 feet (3.4m) long, and it weighs about 5 tons (4.5t). During a test at the museum, the difference engine performed calculations accurate to thirty-one places. Researchers proved that if Babbage had actually built his machine, it would have worked. A second difference engine was completed in 2008. It is on display at the Computer History Museum in Mountain View, California.

A construction of Babbage's Difference Engine No. 2 was completed in 2000 by the Science Museum in London from the designer's original plans.

appeared that he was on the right track, but the project was plagued with political and economic problems. The machine would have had thousands of handcrafted moving parts that would have been very expensive to make so Babbage never completed the first model. Modern researchers who have studied the plans agree that it would have been as big and heavy as a locomotive. The difference engine was never built in Babbage's lifetime. Fortunately, he kept careful records of his ideas in a series of notebooks that he called his scribbling books.

The Analytical Engine

In 1834 Babbage turned his attention to creating the analytical engine. It was capable of a wider range of calculations than his earlier inventions and was designed to analyze a wider range of data. The analytical engine included two elements, a store and a mill, that served a purpose similar to that of the memory and processor of a modern computer. Babbage planned for his machine to be constructed with brass fittings and powered by steam. The operator would feed paper instruction cards into the machine, which would produce results on blank pasteboard cards or metal plates. Babbage predicted that the analytical engine would be capable of completing sixty additions or subtractions and printing the results in one minute. In the same amount of time, it would also be able to multiply two fifty-digit numbers. He even figured out a way for the machine to play chess and

The Analytical Engine, a calculating machine conceived by Babbage in 1834, was not fully constructed in his lifetime. Shown here are the mill and printing portions of the device, built from Babbage's original plans.

tic-tac-toe. Once again, Babbage's creation existed only on paper. Because of the difficulty and expense of producing the parts and a lack of funding, the machine never progressed further than the planning stage.

Making Conversation

One of the issues that Babbage wrestled with was how to give instructions to the analytical engine. He said, "The machine is not a thinking being, but simply an automaton which acts according to the laws imposed upon it."[2] To help solve the problem he recruited Ada Byron (1815–1852), the daughter of the famous British poet, Lord Byron. Babbage called her the enchantress of numbers, because she was more interested in mathematics, patterns, and symbols than in poetry. Byron would later marry a man named William King and become the Countess of Lovelace.

In Tribute

The U.S. Department of Defense computer programming language known as ADA is named in honor of Ada King, Countess of Lovelace. A programming language is a vocabulary and set of rules that allows humans to communicate instructions to machines. In the 1970s the Department of Defense (DOD) employed hundreds of languages for its programming. Most were developed to do specific jobs as part of embedded systems and real-time programs. An embedded system is one that is included within the machine it controls, such as a car, airplane, or stereo. Real-time programs are used to control such things as traffic lights, barcode scanners, and even guided missiles. Real-time programs are those that have a critical response time or deadline that they must meet. For example, the antilock brake system of a car must respond by releasing the brakes before they lock causing an accident. In 1975 the DOD decided to create a single language that it could use for all types of needs, including work with artificial intelligence. The department held a contest and invited several teams of programmers to participate. The winner was a team from the CII Honeywell-Bull company of France, and the winning programming language was named ADA. ADA was originally controlled entirely by the DOD, but in 1987, it was released to the public. ADA is a general-purpose language designed to be readable, easily maintained, and easy to use.

Lady Lovelace was a well-educated woman. In 1842, when Italian engineer Luigi Menabrea wrote a French language review of Babbage's proposed analytical engine, Babbage asked Lady Lovelace to translate the piece into English. Not only did she do as he asked, but she also added her own set of notes. Her notes included the first description of a step-by-step sequence of operations, or stored instructions, for solving mathematical problems. Contemporary computers use a variety of these sets of simple instructions, known as programs, to perform a range of complex functions. Many mathematicians agree that Lady Lovelace's idea would have worked perfectly if the machine had actually been built. Although her method was not tested, it is often referred to as the first computer program and Lady Lovelace is sometimes called the first computer programmer. Even though Babbage and Lady Lovelace set the stage for the development of the computer, it would be a long time before the next step toward an intelligent machine was taken. In fact, much of Babbage's work was forgotten once he died, and other scientists reinvented his ideas decades later. Babbage's notebooks were discovered in 1937, and he was given his rightful place in history as a pioneer in the development of the computer.

Augusta Ada Byron King, the Countess of Lovelace, studied Babbage's plans for the Analytical Engine in 1842 and developed a set of operating instructions that is considered the first computer program.

The Turing Machine and Colossus Code Breaking

The modern computer era began in the twentieth century as scientists gained greater understanding about electrical currents and programming. In 1936 English mathematician Alan Turing (1912–1954) developed plans for the first universal computer. Turing described it as a machine that could be made to do the work of all others. It became known as the universal Turing machine. Turing never built the machine, but the plans included data storage, or memory; a method of computation; and a program that enabled the operator and the machine to communicate. According to the design, an operator would enter input data using a long thin strip of paper. An internal scanner allowed the machine to read the symbols on the paper.

A few years later the onset of World War II changed everything as nation after nation joined the conflict. Turing became a cryptanalyst, or code breaker, at the Government Code and Cypher School at Bletchley Park. Also known as Station X, Bletchley Park was an estate in Buckinghamshire, England. There the British and their allies worked to break secret German communication codes. One of their most valuable tools was the first electronic computer, Colossus, which was built in 1943. Many people took part in designing, building, and operating the Colossus, including mathematician Max Newman (1897–1984), engineer Tommy Flowers (1905–1998) and later engineer Alan Coombs (1911–1995). There were ten computers built and they were top secret. Unlike earlier machines, which used relay switches to control the electrical currents that allowed the machines to process information, the Colossus computers employed smaller, faster vacuum tubes to create or strengthen the electrical current. The processing speed of these computers was advanced, but their only purpose was code breaking and that was all that they were programmed to do.

ENIAC: A Great Brain

The first fully electronic digital computer was the Electronic Numerical Integrator and Computer (ENIAC). Construction started in 1943 in the United States under the code name "Project PX." It was invented by American

BOOLEAN LOGIC

George Boole (1815 – 1864) developed a system of logic in the 1830s and 40s that relies on the use of three basic operators, or "gates" – AND, OR, and, NOT – to interpret information. It was perfect for use in computers because according to the logic, any information could be presented as true or false and so could be presented in a binary system. In the 1930s, mathematician Claude Shannon discovered that electrical circuits could be linked together to process binary code using Boolean Logic.

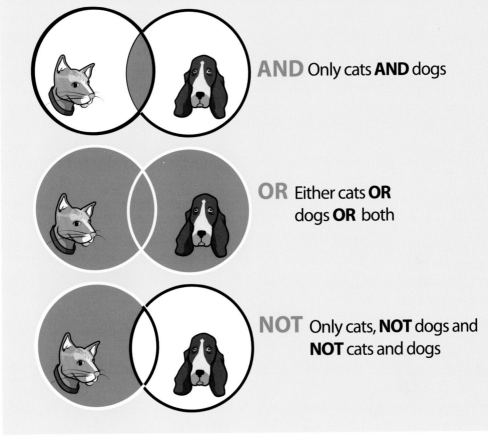

AND Only cats **AND** dogs

OR Either cats **OR** dogs **OR** both

NOT Only cats, **NOT** dogs and **NOT** cats and dogs

Sources: www.le.ac.uk/li/sources/subject3/geol/ist/boolean.html.
http://computer.yourdictionary.com/boolean-logic.

physicist and engineer John W. Mauchly (1907–1980) and American engineer J. Presper Eckert Jr. (1919–1995). The ENIAC was originally designed to calculate tables for the U.S. Army, but it was first used to make calculations for the hydrogen bomb.

When the ENIAC was introduced in 1946, the press quickly nicknamed it the Giant Brain. It was roughly 8 feet (2.4m) tall, 80 feet (24m) long, and weighed nearly 3 tons (2.7t). It was the first machine to use digital circuits and vacuum tube relays for computing, which made it about one thousand times faster than earlier electromechanical machines. The previous machines interpreted numbers by reading the number of electrical pulses. For example, the number ten was communicated by ten pulses. Digital circuits allowed the ENIAC to read the number ten from just one electrical pulse that came from the tens-digit circuit. The ENIAC could read the number thirty-two from three pulses from the tens circuit and two pulses from the ones circuit rather than thirty-two individual pulses.

Earlier machines were designed to solve a particular set of problems and that was all they could do. One of the greatest advances the ENIAC represented was the capability of being reprogrammed to solve a wide range of computing problems, which made it the first general-purpose electronic computer. The ENIAC's designers went on to form a company called the Eckert-Mauchly Computer Corporation. In partnership with mathematician, John von Neumann (1903–1957) they produced some of the best-known early computers, including the Electronic Discrete Variable Automatic Computer (EDVAC) and the Universal Automatic Computer (UNIVAC), which became the world's first large-scale commercial computer.

By the end of the 1940s, computers could reliably perform a wide range of tasks and complete hundreds of calculations per second. Such speed and accuracy was a huge step forward on the path to AI. The next step was to create a machine that could learn. In 1947, Alan Turing proposed the possibility of a machine with a mechanism for altering its own program if it was not achieving success, meaning it could learn from experience. Turing illustrated his ideas on machine intelligence by using chess. In 1948, he wrote, but did not publish, a report titled *Intelligent Machinery*. In it he introduces the concept of training a network of artificial neurons, or brain cells, to perform particular tasks much the way that the human brain is taught to do certain tasks. Turing later said, "I believe that at the end of the [twentieth] century the use of words and general educated opinion will have altered so much that one will be able to speak of machines thinking without expecting to be contradicted."[3]

Machines That Learn

In order to learn a person must be able to gather and process new information. To create machines that could learn, scientists and engineers needed to figure out how to pack more information into smaller spaces. Most early electrical computers, like the ENIAC, ran on large vacuum tubes that passed electrical charges from one to another. The glowing glass tubes would often overheat and fail. They attracted moths, which could cause a computer to break down if the bug became trapped between relays. This may have led to the use of the term *bug*, to describe a problem in a computer. Another issue was that a machine powered by thousands of vacuum tubes was often so big that it could weigh tons and fill an entire room.

All that changed with the development of the transistor in 1947 at the Bell Telephone Laboratories in New Jersey. The three physicists who created this breakthrough, John Bardeen (1908–1991), William Shockley (1910–1989), and Walter Brattain (1902–1987), were awarded the Nobel Prize in Physics in 1956 for their achievement. A transistor is a tiny electric switch made of silicon. Researchers found a way to embed transistors and other tiny components in chips of silicon. Each chip is a small electronic circuit, also known as an integrated circuit, used to transmit electronic data signals. The chips were small, inexpensive, easy to produce, and reliable. They led to the creation of machines that were not only smaller, but also faster and much more powerful. By the

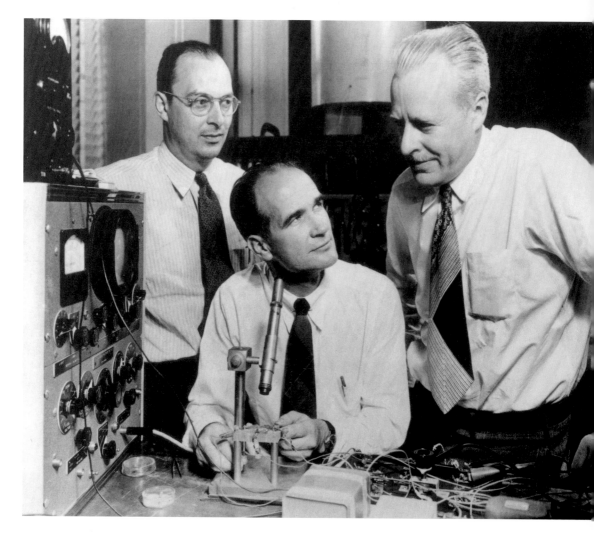

Nobel Prize winners, from left, John Bardeen, William Shockley, and Walter Brattain were American physicists who invented the transistor in 1947.

1960s, it became possible to embed thousands of transistors and other components on each chip. By the early twenty-first century, millions of bits of information could fit on a microchip the size of a grain of rice.

As computers became more powerful, scientists searched for a way to determine if they had reached the level of human intelligence. Turing proposed that if a machine can act as intelligently as a human, then it is as intelligent as a human. In 1950 he developed the Turing Test, a method for assessing computer intelligence. The test requires a computer and

Speaking in Code

Computers communicate in a mathematical language called binary code. In the 1940s the work of mathematicians Claude Shannon and John von Neumann showed that a binary system was the best choice for programming computers. In a binary code, information is represented by two values, 0 and 1. These values can be combined in different ways to represent any number or letter. A bit is a digit in the binary number system, and it may have a value of 0 or 1. Stored in the computer memory, each bit is a small electrical switch that is either off for a value of 0 or on for a value of 1. Bits are arranged in groups of eight called a byte. Strings of binary digits represent letters and numbers. Each byte may represent up to 256 values. Shannon figured out how electrical circuits could be linked together to process binary code using a system of logic called Boolean Logic. George Boole (1815–1864) had developed the logic in the 1800s. It was perfect for use in computers, because according to the logic, any information could be presented as true or false and so could be presented in a binary system.

two human participants in separate rooms. One person uses a keyboard to ask questions of the other two participants and a screen to read the text-only answers. The goal is for the questioner to determine by the answers which of the other two participants is the computer and which is the human. The questioner may ask anything, even "Are you a computer?" The computer is permitted to give a false or incorrect response to convince the questioner that it is the human. If a computer is able to fool a number of questioners, it can be considered an intelligent, thinking machine. No AI program has yet convincingly passed the Turing Test, but computers have proved capable of performing a wide range of intelligent tasks, including playing chess.

Early AI Programs

Checkers and chess require players to plan moves, use strategy, and consider the moves that an opponent might choose, making the games ideal for testing AI programs.

World chess champion Garry Kasparov, left, played a series of games against IBM's Deep Blue computer in 1996, winning the six-game match; Deep Blue's architect and designer, Feng-Hsuing Hsu, is at right. A year later, an upgraded Deep Blue defeated Kasparov in a series rematch.

American mathematical engineer Claude Shannon (1916–2001) designed a chess-playing program but never tested it. He said, "Although perhaps of no practical importance, the question [of whether a computer can be programmed to play chess] is of theoretical interest, and it is hoped that a satisfactory solution of this problem will act as a wedge in attacking other problems of a similar nature and of greater significance."[4]

In 1951 British computer scientist Christopher Strachey (1916–1975) coded a checkers program for a model of Turing's automatic computing engine, but it did not run successfully. Strachey tried again with a Ferranti Mark I computer and was pleased to report that the machine was able to play a complete game. Chess proved to be more challenging. As Strachey made progress with checkers, tweintieth-century research scientist Dietrich Prinz created a chess program for the same computer. It instructed the machine to consider every possible move and choose the best course. The machine was much slower than a human, and it was able to find the best moves only when the player was two moves away from checkmate.

The first AI program to run in the United States was a checkers program written in 1952 by Arthur Samuel (1901–1990) for an IBM computer. Samuel helped the computer to improve its play by installing two copies of the program, Alpha and Beta, into the same machine. Alpha and Beta played against each other over and over again. The program ranked moves and board positions based on their rate of success. As the game progressed, it made changes to Alpha's ranking method but left Beta as it was. If Alpha appeared to be playing poorly after making an adjustment, the program dropped the changes. If Alpha's play improved, the program kept the changes and made the same corrections to Beta. Over many games the computer became a better player. By 1955 it was able to beat Samuel in a game. In 1962 it won a

BITS & BYTES
18 billion
Amount of dollars invested in industrial robots worldwide in 2007.

game against a former checkers champion. The human player went on to win the next six games, but it was clear that the program was learning.

In 1989 IBM took up the challenge to build a computer that could play chess well enough to beat a human champion. Reigning world chess champion Garry Kasparov played against and beat the computer, called Deep Blue, in 1996. Although Deep Blue did win one game, Kasparov won the six-game match. IBM upgraded the machine and a rematch took place on May 11, 1997. Deep Blue beat Kasparov in a six-game match. They played three tie games, and the computer won two out of the other three games. Deep Blue could examine 200 million possible moves per second, and it could look ahead as many as fourteen plays. Kasparov even commented that he saw deep intelligence and creativity in some of the machines moves. It was the first and only time a world chess champion was defeated by a computer.

The Learning Machine: Weak AI

Game-playing computers are examples of weak artificial intelligence. Weak AI is a computer-based AI that can solve problems or apply reason in a limited way. Shopper was one of the first AI programs to try learning a skill other than a game. In 1952 it ran on the EDSAC computer at the University of Cambridge in England. The program was presented with a simulated minimall of eight different shops. It was then instructed to buy a certain product. Shopper searched each shop for the target item, storing information about other products during the search, not unlike a human shopper. Each shopping trip became faster and more efficient as the program figured out where to find a variety of items. Eventually, it could go to the correct shop every time and find the needed product immediately. This is called rote learning, or learning by repetition. Students often use this method to memorize multiplication tables or scientific principles. Although it is a form of learning, rote learning is not the same as developing a deep understanding of the facts. Shopper was an early form of applied AI, also known as advanced information processing. The goal of such programs is to produce smart systems, such as medical diagnosis systems, stock-trading systems, and security systems that are able to recognize faces. Such systems are extremely helpful in the workplace, but they cannot be defined as truly intelligent.

A machine that demonstrates weak AI may be faster and more reliable than humans and may perform tasks that require simple elements of intelligence, such as the ability to learn by rote, or repetition. That does not mean that the machine has a conscious mind. That is the domain of strong AI—AI that meets or exceeds human intelligence.

The Thinking Machine: Strong AI

To exhibit strong AI, a machine would have to be able to perceive and process changing information from its surroundings, think abstractly, reason, solve problems, and show awareness of its existence and its place in its environment. The mission to define and develop strong AI was addressed in 1956 at the Dartmouth Artificial Intelligence Conference at Dartmouth College. Some of the most respected names in the new science gathered at the New Hampshire campus. During the conference, scientist Herbert Simon (1916–2001) predicted that within twenty years machines would be capable of doing any work a man could do. He and many of those who attended the conference accepted the bold statement known as the Dartmouth Proposal: "Every aspect of learning or any other feature of intelligence can in principle be so precisely described that a machine can be made to simulate it."[5]

Although the creation of strong AI is exciting, some well-known scientists doubt that it is possible. In 1980, John Searle (1932–), a professor of philosophy at the University of California, Berkeley, proposed an argument against it called the Chinese Room. According to the argument, a person who understands only English is in a locked room. In the room are some sheets of paper and a book about Chinese writing that is written in English. Someone slides a piece of paper under the door, and on it is a puzzle written in Chinese. The person in the room follows the English language instructions in the book that show which Chinese symbols to write on the paper. Without knowing what they mean, the person in the room writes the symbols and passes the paper back under the door. To the person outside the room, it appears that the person inside reads and writes Chinese and was able to solve the puzzle. In fact that person was just following the English language instructions in the book and has no idea what the answer means. Searle's point is that although a computer may appear to be solving problems, it is just following a program, and it does not understand the meaning of the answers. Searle explains that a computer is only imitating thought. He says, "No one supposes that computer simulations of a five-alarm fire will burn the neighborhood down or that a computer simulation of a rainstorm will leave us all drenched."[6]

Drew McDermott, professor of computer science at Yale University in Connecticut, disagrees. Using the chess-playing computer Deep Blue as an example, McDermott points out that, "saying Deep Blue doesn't really think about chess is like saying an airplane doesn't really fly because it doesn't flap its wings."[7]

As the twenty-first century begins, the debate about the possibility of strong AI continues in universities and laboratories around the world. Meanwhile many continue to work toward a future that may include thinking machines. To make the leap from computers that do only what they are programmed to do to intelligent machines that think for themselves, researchers must first agree on the definition of intelligence and understand how it works.

CHAPTER 2

Creating an Intelligent Machine

The computers of the early twenty-first century are capable of performing a wide range of tasks at amazing speeds and with incredible accuracy, but most of these computers work under known conditions. This means that they are programmed to deal with the situations that they would be expected to encounter while doing the job that they are instructed to do. True intelligence demands more. An intelligent machine needs to have the ability to learn about its environment and adjust as that environment changes. It should be able to deal with unexpected conditions. Hod Lipson, a professor of mechanical and aerospace engineering at Cornell University in New York, explains, "The less we can foresee issues, the more we will need machines to adapt and make decisions on their own." He adds, "As machines get better at learning how to learn, I think that leads down the path to consciousness and self-awareness."[8]

What Is Intelligence?

When trying to define intelligence, scientists agree that the only thing they agree on is that the exact definition is still open to debate. In 1994 fifty-two researchers contributed to a report titled *Mainstream Science on Intelligence*. In it they describe intelligence as "a very general mental capability that, among other things, involves the ability to reason, plan, solve problems, think abstractly, comprehend complex ideas, learn quickly and learn from experience."[9]

Scientists have also identified different kinds of intelligence, such as natural intelligence (NI) and general intelligence, that are relevant to the field of AI. NI researchers focus on intelligence and the human brain as part of a biological system. They study all of the elements that might influence behavior in living things, including the environment where

Multiple Intelligences

One definition of intelligence is the ability to learn from experience, reason, plan, solve problems, and apply and communicate what has been learned. Intelligence tests mainly measure a person's ability and skill using math, reading, and writing. Educators think that this method of measuring intelligence is too narrow, because people think and learn in different ways. Howard Gardner (1943–), a professor of education, suggests that there are eight different types of human intelligence:

1. Verbal-linguistic intelligence is the ability to use both spoken and written language to express complex meaning. Writers, journalists, and public speakers display this type of intelligence.
2. Logical-mathematical intelligence is the ability to reason and carry out complex mathematical operations and recognize abstract patterns.
3. Visual-spatial intelligence is the ability to visualize a three-dimensional environment or to imagine a setting or draw a map.
4. Bodily-kinesthetic intelligence is the ability to use physical skills to express ideas and feelings, or to create or transform things by hand. Artists, dancers, and athletes display this type of intelligence.
5. Musical-rhythmic intelligence is the ability to recognize elements of sound, including pitch, melody, rhythm, and tone.
6. Interpersonal intelligence is the ability to understand, interact with, motivate, and lead others. Politicians, teachers, and social workers display this type of intelligence.
7. Intrapersonal intelligence is the ability to understand oneself. Psychologists, spiritual leaders, and philosophers display this type of intelligence.
8. Naturalist intelligence is the capacity to understand the natural environment and to recognize relationships in nature.

those beings live. AI researchers have noted that a thinking machine would also be influenced by its environment and would have to be able to adapt to changes in that environment.

Scientist Francis Galton (1822–1911) was among the first to propose a theory of general intelligence that could be measured with tests. General intelligence is divided into two categories. Verbal intelligence is the ability to analyze information using language and skills, such as reading and writing. Nonverbal intelligence is the ability to analyze information using visual skills and reasoning.

In 2009 a team of researchers from several universities reported that they had mapped the parts of the brain that affect general intelligence. They found that a network of regions across both sides of the brain is involved, and the brain's ability to establish connections between the regions turned out to be what is most important. Neuroscientist Jan Gläscher notes, "General intelligence depends on the brain's ability to integrate, to pull together, several different kinds of processing, such as working memory."[10] The verbal and nonverbal elements of general intelligence, as well as the ability of the human brain to make connections, are important factors of human intelligence being studied by AI researchers.

A Bottom-Up Approach

Some researchers think that the path to an intelligent machine may lie in a better understanding of Earth's insects. Insects may not be capable of higher thought, but they are able to survive in their environment. They can find food and shelter, avoid predators, and find mates. Social insects, such as ants and bees, recognize threats in their environment and work together to adapt to changing circumstances. The ability to accomplish such simple things would be an amazing leap for a machine. A growing number of studies show that certain species of insects can count, categorize objects, and

THE HUMAN MODEL FOR INTELLIGENCE

One of the challenges to creating a true AI is developing a system that can mimic the complicated array of brain structures that contribute to human intelligence and self-awareness.

1. **Frontal lobe** – controls learning, planning, reasoning, decision-making, and some aspects of speech.
2. **Temporal lobe** – controls memory, hearing, and emotion.
3. **Parietal lobe** – controls sense of touch.
4. **Occipital lobe** – controls sight and perception.
5. **Cerebellum** – controls coordination and balance.

Source: NATIONAL GEOGRAPHIC EXPLORER! Jan./Feb. 2007, Vol. 6, No. 4, p 20.

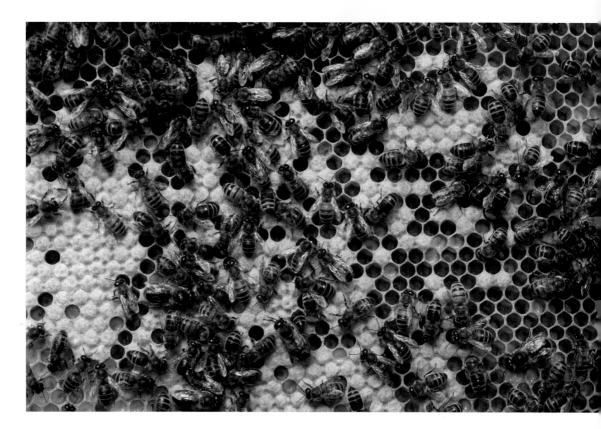

Honeybees work together in their hive. Some researchers believe that studies of the brains of social insects like the honeybee can reveal much about the nature of intelligence.

recognize landmarks. As a model for building an intelligent machine, many scientists view the insect brain as an excellent starting point.

Researchers admit that the size of a brain is not the best measure of how smart a creature might be. Large brains tend to have a lot of backups, or repetition of the same sets of neuronal, or nerve, circuits. A better measure of intelligence is the complexity of connections between brain cells. Figuring out how a fairly small number of cells work together to process complex problems could lead to computers that could do some of the same tasks that humans do but faster and more efficiently. In fact, in a Discovery News article, author Emily Sohns notes that scientists have calculated that "a few thousand neurons could support consciousness."[11] If that is true, then smaller, less-complicated insect brains that are made up of under a million neurons would be good models for machine intelligence. Computer scientist Greg Fish points out that they could show how certain processes are done on a basic level, and researchers "may learn something about the evolution of intelligence."[12]

A 3-D Rat

The brain of a rat is much more complex than that of an insect, and a supercomputer is giving scientists a peek into how it works. Blue Brain is a 3-D computer image designed to imitate a slice of a rat's brain. The simulated slice contains about ten thousand neurons and 30 million synaptic connections. "This is the first model of the brain that has been built from the bottom-up," says Henry Markram, a neuroscientist and director of the Blue Brain project. "There are lots of models out there, but this is the only one that is totally biologically accurate. We began with the most basic facts about the brain and just worked from there."[13]

Blue Brain was created by a team of researchers at the École Polytechnique Fédérale de Lausanne in Switzerland. The simulation is created by an IBM supercomputer that performs 22.8 trillion operations per second. When the project began in 2005, the virtual neurons fired only when acted upon by a simulated electrical current. Now the virtual neurons have begun to organize themselves into a more complex pattern that resembles a wave moving from one side of the virtual brain to the other. According to the researchers, "this is the beginning of the self-organizing brain patterns that eventually, in more complex mammal brains, become personality."[14] Researchers hope to use the information to create a digital human brain in the near future.

Mimicking the Human Brain

The human brain is an amazing neural network that connects more than 100 billion brain cells called neurons. These interconnected cells shuttle both chemical and electrical signals throughout the brain. Individual neurons

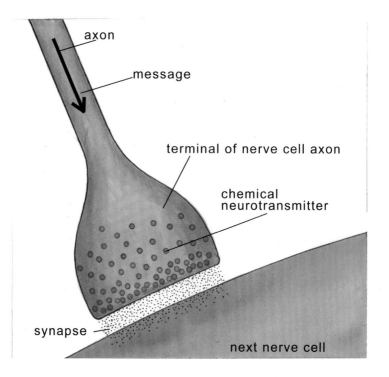

A diagram illustrates the path of signals through the brain's neural network. Messages travel through the axon to the synapse, where chemical transmitters send the signal to the next nerve cell.

axon

message

terminal of nerve cell axon

chemical neurotransmitter

synapse

next nerve cell

receive signals through specialized structures called dendrites, which extend from one end of each neuron. Dendrites send the signals they collect to the soma, a large central part of each neuron where information is processed. This information is made up of two main kinds of signals. One kind tells the neuron to speed up its signaling, and the other kind tells it to slow down. In the soma, these signals are added together and help the neuron decide what kind of signal it should send. Once this decision is made, the neuron sends out its own signal, instructing other neurons to either speed up or slow down. This signal is sent out through another part of the neuron called the axon. Axons are thin fibers that reach out and almost touch neighboring cells. Between the end of each axon and its target cell is a small gap called a synapse. The end of each axon releases chemical signals into the synapse, and these instruct the target cell to either speed up or slow down. In this way the signals pass from one neuron to the next until a stop signal prevents the process from continuing. The brain is

Inside an MRI Machine

AI researchers often use computer models to help them understand the nature of intelligence. Until the early 1990s, it was difficult to directly observe a thinking brain at work. The functioning magnetic resonance imaging (fMRI) scanner has changed that. This instrument enables scientists to study brain activity without using tools that enter the body.

During a regular MRI scan, a person lies inside a machine that contains a powerful magnet. Electric coils produce variations in the magnetic field at different points. When the nuclei of hydrogen atoms are caught in this strong magnetic field, they line up. A pulse of radio waves is used to make them change direction. As they return to the original position, they give off energy in the form of a radio wave, which is used to create an image.

An fMRI is a special type of test that shows which parts of the brain is active when a person performs certain mental tasks, such as viewing pictures, smelling odors, or listening to sounds. The scanner detects the increase in blood flow to the most active parts of the brain during the task and creates a 3-D map of the brain.

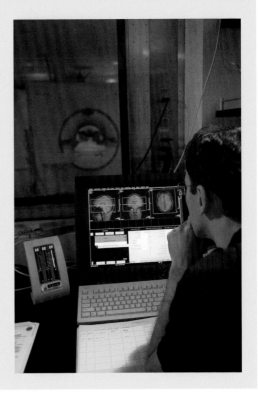

A researcher studies brain images transmitted from a functional magnetic resonance imaging (fMRI) scanner.

continuously firing and rewiring itself. Although scientists are still attempting to understand exactly how learning works in the human brain, they know that when neurons fire over and over again in a particular pattern, that pattern becomes stronger.

As complex as the human brain is, many scientists believe that it can one day be duplicated. Marvin Minsky (1927–), a professor of computer science, is one of the pioneers of AI and cofounder of the Computer Science and Artificial Intelligence Laboratory at the Massachusetts Institute of Technology (MIT) in Cambridge, Massachusetts. According to Minsky, "if the nervous system obeys the laws of physics and chemistry, which we have every reason to suppose it does, then we ought to be able to reproduce the behavior of the nervous system with some physical device."[15]

Connectionism

To mimic the human brain, scientists had to find a way to mimic the interconnected neural network. In 1943 neurophysiologist Warren McCulloch (1898–1969) and mathematician Walter Pitts (1923–1969) published a paper that includes the first mathematical model of a neural network. The scientists compare the brain to a computer and each neuron to a simple digital processor. The paper established a foundation for a branch of AI research called connectionism. It is based on the idea that computer programs can simulate the same connections that are found in the brain and that these virtual connections, known as artificial neuron networks (ANNs), are good models of human intelligence.

In artificial neuron networks, the artificial neurons, or units, are organized in layers. The units have connections that serve the same purpose as the synapses of physical neurons. They receive and send information. To indicate the importance of any incoming signals from a given input, the program assigns each input a weight that is a fraction between one and zero. The sum of all incoming weights equals the net value of the unit.

Before a unit will fire and send a signal to the next unit, its net value must reach a certain number. This number is called an activation value. The input weights can be raised or lowered by the program. The scientist instructs the program how to translate the incoming information into output information. Over time the network connections become weaker or stronger much the way they do in the human brain. These networks are good at recognizing patterns. Because of this, ANN software can be used to translate languages, compare fingerprints, and analyze handwriting. Some police departments use an ANN search engine called Coplink, a powerful AI software application. It searches case files and criminal databases, uncovering hidden relationships and associations of criminals. The software indirectly helps to lower crime rates while saving police valuable time, money, and resources. In fact, Coplink was used to help solve a famous case in the Washington D.C.–area in 2002. During three weeks in October, two individuals shot and killed or injured thirteen people. Coplink was used to analyze the data about the crimes and it connected a specific vehicle to the area of two shootings. The white van was owned by one of two men who police had already arrested and so helped connect the men to the crime. Coplink is one example of an AI application that is known as an expert system.

Expert Systems

An expert system is a computer program that is designed to support the work of experts in fields such as medicine and finance. The system simulates the judgment of a human expert. Designed in 1965, Dendral is considered the first expert system. It contained a remarkable store of information about organic chemistry and was able to automate part of the decision-making and problem-solving processes for the chemists who used it.

There are two parts to an expert system: the knowledge base and the logic program, or inference engine. To build the system, a knowledge engineer interviews experts in the field and enters the information into the computer, creating the knowledge base. The person using the expert system enters their observations and any additional facts about a given problem. The logic program uses the observations and searches the knowledge base to suggest probable answers.

Deduction and inference are two forms of logic that can be used to analyze observations. Deductive logic uses a general rule to explain a specific observation. Detectives typically use deductive thinking to interpret evidence. Many AI applications are based purely on deductive logic. In contrast, inference builds on patterns among observations to create new general rules. Scientists employ inference to create new theories about how the world works. Advanced expert systems employ inference to establish new rules to predict outcomes. Expert systems can process thousands of new facts and observations to create original rules and make predictions. A person using these systems must exercise common sense and remember that they are only tools that suggest probabilities. Nonetheless, expert systems are good examples of how AI is being used to provide technical support in the modern workplace.

Artificial Senses

Expert systems generally rely on data that is originally entered by a knowledge engineer. Other types of systems

A robot performs assembly work on a Jeep Grand Cherokee at Chrysler's Jefferson North Assembly Plant in Detroit, Michigan, one of many applications of robot technology in modern factories.

HAL and *Deep Space 1*

One of the greatest science-fiction villains is a computer that takes control of the *Discovery One* spacecraft on a mission to Jupiter and kills the crew. The computer, a character in the 1968 film *2001: A Space Odyssey*, the HAL 9000 (heuristically programmed algorithmic computer) is an example of strong AI. It recognizes and reacts to its environment, interacts verbally with the crew, and maintains all of the spacecraft's systems. When HAL appears to malfunction, the astronauts try to shut it down. Hal chooses to save itself by disconnecting the spacecraft's life support system.

In 1998 NASA launched the spacecraft, *Deep Space 1* on a mission to test new technologies in space. Although there were no human astronauts onboard, the craft was equipped with a variety of AI systems that could make decisions. For example, the autonomous navigation system kept *Deep Space 1* on course by comparing its position to certain stars and asteroids. The craft used software called Remote Agent to determine how to meet goals that scientists programmed into it. Finally, *Deep Space 1* sent messages back to Earth, such as "All is well" or "Help needed." *Deep Space 1* successfully completed its mission and was retired in 2001.

rely on sensors. There are many examples of weak or narrow AI in daily life, including global positioning systems (GPS) in cars and even thermostats in homes and offices. These systems are programmed to sense or perceive something, such as position or a temperature. Artificial perception is based on feedback theory developed by mathematician Norbert Wiener (1894–1964). He proposed that intelligent behavior, real or artificial, is the result of feedback mechanisms, where behavior is based on sensory input. Intelligent beings must be able to sense their environment to determine an appropriate intelligent response. A person has five senses that gather information about the outside world and send it to the brain. Artificial perception is based on this concept. Although they are not truly intelligent, weak AI systems must also have a way to collect information about the environment. Sensors gather information for machines. A thermostat that monitors the temperature of a house has a sensor to measure the actual temperature, a program that allows it to compare the actual temperature to the desired temperature set by the homeowner, and a program that allows it to control the central air system of the house. When a homeowner sets a desired temperature for the furnace, for example, the thermostat can tell the furnace when the temperature inside the house drops below the desired temperature, and the furnace turns on and remains on until the thermostat tells it that the house has returned to the desired temperature.

Machines with visual sensors are often used on assembly lines in factories. One of these robots, named Freddy, was built at the University of Edinburgh in Scotland in the late 1960s and was composed of only a single eye and a claw-like hand. In robots like Freddy, the eyes are actually digital cameras that send images to a computer for processing. Freddy could not move from place to place, but it could rotate its eye and grip with its hand. The robot was programmed to recognize many objects and assemble a toy car from a pile of parts. Modern factories use robots like Freddy to perform assembly and quality control. Machine vision is also used to process farm products by detecting poor quality food in a process called optical sorting. Visual sensors are also extremely important in the military where they are used on missile guidance systems and navigation systems. Modern robots are often equipped with GPS; video cameras; array microphones, which can distinguish a voice from background noise; and many additional sensors.

Natural Language Processing

Gathering sensory information is a critical step for many systems that employ AI. Communicating that information is

Upgrade: Your Thought Is My Command

Researchers at the Honda Research Institute of Japan may have found a way to eliminate the need to use spoken language to communicate with an artificial intelligence. They have developed a brain machine interface (BMI) that allows a person to control a robot by human thought alone. When a human thinks, tiny electrical and blood flow changes occur in the brain. The noninvasive BMI device measures and analyzes the changes, using electroencephalography (EEG) to measure electrical impulse and near-infrared spectroscopy (NIRS) to measure blood flow through tiny vessels in the scalp. Sensors are placed on the head of the user, who then imagines moving a body part. The result is transmitted to a nearby robot that then moves its corresponding body part. Tests have produced an accuracy rate of up to 90 percent. The goal of the research is to build a robot that can function by human thought alone.

equally important. Humans usually communicate by speaking and writing. Natural language processing (NLP) enables machines to read and understand human language. Voice-recognition programs can identify words quite well, but it is harder to build a machine that can understand what those words mean in context. This is a challenging task, because the meaning of a sentence may often be difficult to interpret. Barbara Grosz, a computer scientist at Harvard University in Massachusetts, notes, "Regarding language as communication requires consideration of what is said (literally), what is intended, and the relationship between the two."[16]

There are many benefits to interacting with a computer using a spoken language. The interaction between an operator and a computer is much simpler if the person can ask questions or give instructions without having to enter them

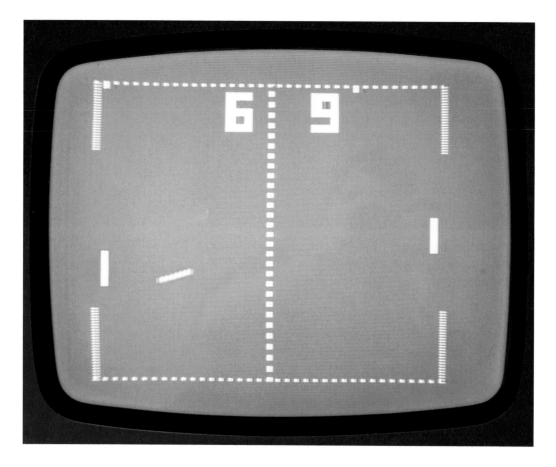

Primitive by today's gaming standards, Pong was the first commercially successful video game.

on a keyboard. NLP also offers scientists a way to study how humans process language, offering clues to intelligence. Researchers in the field of natural language processing are making great strides. For example, practical applications in everyday life include information retrieval and automatic language translators that allow people who speak different languages to interact directly without the help of a human interpreter.

An important goal for the future is to have the computer understand natural language well enough to learn on its own by reading from sources on the Internet. This would be a tremendous leap toward the goal of achieving strong AI. Joseph Weizenbaum (1923–2008), formerly a professor at the Computer Science and Artificial Intelligence Laboratory at MIT, described the ultimate goal of strong AI as being "nothing less than to build a machine on the model of man, a robot that is to have its childhood, to learn language as a child does, to gain its knowledge of the world by sensing the world through its own organs, and ultimately to contemplate the whole domain of human thought."[17]

AI in Gaming

Elements such as artificial perception and natural language processing can make AI-related programs easier to use in daily life. Gaming is an extremely popular area of software programming that benefits from such advances in AI. The original video gaming system was designed in 1966 by engineer Ralph Baer.

Pong, based on the game of table tennis, was one of the first commercially successful video games. It was created by a young engineer named Allan Alcorn and released in 1972. Young people flocked to video arcades to play the game, which allowed them to play against another person or against the computer. As of the early twenty-first century, computer and video games constituted a rapidly growing, billion-dollar industry. Whether they are used for education or for entertainment, the quality and diversity of game content is growing too. In many of the most popular games, adaptive AI agents interact with the player by taking on the role of an opponent or a teammate. Video games rely on the ability to teach adaptive AI agents to respond to changes in action, environment, and the strategy of the human player. Designers use AI agents to create characters that react to the game player's actions in a fairly unpredictable way. AI researchers note that one element of human intelligence is the ability to adapt to changing situations. These games are an excellent way to examine how machine intelligence can learn to deal with such situations. The future will offer researchers a wider range of opportunities to test AI agents as games incorporate such upgrades as 3-D and advanced motion-sensor systems. Ben Goertzel of Novamente, a company that develops artificial general intelligence technology, says, "Due to the explosion of work in 3D gaming, the potential now exists to inexpensively create 3D simulation worlds for AGI [artificial general intelligence] systems to live and interact in."[18] Goertzel points out that AI in an artificial world is as effective at creating a realistic experience as AI in a robot, but without the cost and hassle of creating and maintaining physical robotics.

CHAPTER 3

Intelligent Robots

The most basic forms of artificial intelligence (AI) are computer programs that solve specific problems, but few forms of AI spark the imagination more than the robot. AI of varying levels has been applied in the science of robotics to make life easier and safer for human beings in many ways, and robots are quickly becoming more commonplace. In fact, modern robots come in so many forms, shapes, and sizes that a person may have contact with one without realizing it. Joseph Engelberger (1925–), a pioneer in industrial robotics, once remarked, "I can't define a robot, but I know one when I see one."[19]

A robot is AI in a physical form designed to interact in some way with its environment. According to Nicholas Roy, of the Computer Science and Artificial Intelligence Laboratory at the Massachusetts Institute of Technology, robots might be described as, "AI systems embedded in space and time."[20] Such machines and mechanical devices may display human-like skill in a wide range of tasks. Robots are used on assembly lines to build cars and trucks. They explore the far reaches of space and the depths of the oceans. They also assist doctors during surgery, clean swimming pools and rain gutters, and remind people to take their medicine.

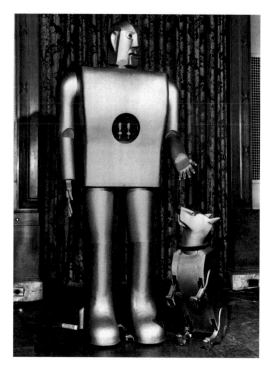

Elektro the robot and his dog Sparko, created by Westinghouse Electric Corporation, were featured at the World's Fair in New York City in 1939 and 1940.

Mechanical Pioneers

The term *robot* entered the English language in 1923. It comes from *robota*, a Czech word that means "drudgery" or "slave-like labor." Czech playwright Karel Capek first used *robota* to describe artificial humanoid workers in his play *Rossum's Universal Robots*.

It was not long before the general public became fascinated with the idea of mechanical beings that could walk and talk. A huge, golden, robotic man named Elektro was a popular attraction at the 1939–1940 New York World's Fair. The robot was a project of Westinghouse Electric Corporation. Elektro was 7 feet (2.1m) tall, and weighed about 265 pounds (120kg). It relied on a combination of motors, photoelectric cells, and telephone relays to enable it to perform twenty-six programmed tasks. Each routine was prompted by special voice commands from a human partner. Elektro did not actually understand the voice commands. It was programmed to respond to patterns of speech, such as the number of syllables spoken. Elektro could raise and lower its arms, turn its head, move its mouth, count on its fingers, blow up a balloon, and even smoke a cigarette and blow out the smoke. The robot moved very slowly across the stage by means of rollers on its feet, but it had to drag a heavy electrical cable behind it. The crowds were still amazed by its performance. Elektro was joined in 1940 by a robot dog named Sparko. The metallic dog could sit up and slowly follow a light source.

Elektro was designed to entertain audiences and was restricted to a stage. In 1948 and 1949, William Grey Walter (1910–1977), of the Burden Neurological Institute in Bristol, England, created the first autonomous, or self-directed, robots. Named Elmer and Elsie, they looked a little like three-wheeled turtles, and they could move around and explore their environment without human guidance. Elmer and Elsie were equipped with light sensors and were attracted to bright sources of light. The sensors enabled them to be aware of and to avoid obstacles in their path. Each robot had the equivalent of two nerve cells, but they were able to accomplish some complex behavior, such as finding their recharging station, when they became low on battery power.

Unimates

Auto manufacturers became the first to use robots in the workplace. In 1961 the Unimates joined the assembly line at a General Motors plant in New Jersey. George Devol (1912–) and Joseph Engelberger created the industrial robots in 1958. The Unimates were 4,000-pound (1,814kg) metal arms that were hydraulically powered and programmed to move in precise repeating patterns. Following commands stored on a magnetic drum, they were flexible enough to perform a number of jobs. They were designed for handling parts weighing up to 500 pounds (227kg). Unimates could weld auto parts with great accuracy. Unlike people, the Unimates did not get tired of doing the same thing over and over, and they could not be injured on the job or harmed by toxic materials. The main problem with the robotic arms was that they were built for a single purpose or group of purposes, and they could not adapt to new tasks. Another issue was that many angry human workers felt that their jobs were being lost to mindless piles of metal. In fact, robots did replace humans in certain jobs. Despite these concerns, industrial robots like Unimate continue to be in use in the twenty-first century. They are reliable and easy-to-operate, and they have become the most widely used industrial robots in the world.

Shakey the Robot

Shakey the robot debuted in 1966 and was the first mobile robot controlled by AI. It was named for the way it trembled and shook as it moved. The robot was built in

California at the Stanford Research Institute, now known as SRI International. It traveled on wheels at about 6 feet (1.8m) per hour, and it had bump detectors at the base. Its head was equipped for artificial perception with a television camera and a range finder, an instrument used to estimate the distance between the robot and other objects. The robot had limited language capability. It did not speak, but it acted on English language commands typed into its computer, and the computer could send a response. Shakey was driven by a problem-solving program called STRIPS. Unlike earlier robots, Shakey was often given general instructions for a particular task and was allowed to figure out how to accomplish the job. In 2004, Shakey was inducted into the Robot Hall of Fame, located at Carnegie Mellon University in Pittsburgh, Pennsylvania.

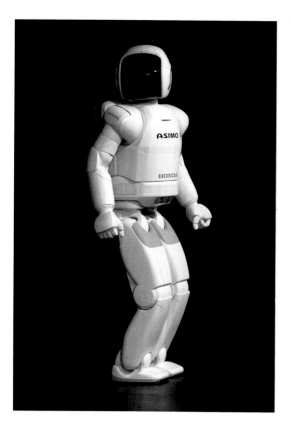

ASIMO, a robot introduced in the early 2000s by Honda Robotics, can walk, climb steps, and perform a variety of simple tasks.

AI in Motion

The robots of the early twenty-first century are far more sophisticated than Shakey. Many are created to not only think like humans, but also to mimic their physical abilities, such as gripping objects and moving freely. A step in this direction is the development of the robotic hand. The human hand is muscular, precise, strong, flexible, and extremely sensitive. Most people give little thought to the fact that slicing an apple, drawing a picture, and carrying a baby are all amazing feats. Modern robotic hands, however, can both pick up an egg without breaking it and crush a walnut in its shell. To accomplish this, robotic hands are often powered by extremely precise stepper motors, which allow the hand to use a range of grasp pressure. The Shadow Hand,

Skin Deep

One obstacle in the development of a human-like robot has been that robots cannot feel pressure or touch objects in the way that humans do. Engineers at the University of California, Berkeley, have developed a new technology that may change that. It is a synthetic electronic skin called e-skin, and it can detect pressure similar to that needed to perform jobs, such as washing dishes or typing on a keyboard. When covered with the electronic skin, robots would be able to touch and move objects with the appropriate force for the task. The strong and flexible e-skin is created using semiconductor nanowires more than ten thousand times thinner than a single human hair. Made from germanium and silicon, the wires are rolled onto a sticky film. Transistors are layered on top, and the final layer is a flexible, pressure-sensitive rubber with pixels that act as switches. Touching the e-skin causes the rubber to deform, which activates the switch of one of the pixels. The next step in the development of e-skin will be to integrate a computer chip to interpret the information from the switches. The e-skin may also benefit humans by restoring the sense of touch for people with replacement limbs. Instead of a computer chip, the electronic skin could interface directly with the human brain.

from the Shadow Robot Company in England, has integrated sensors on its palm and fingers. It has a bank of forty soft "muscles" that operate on compressed air. The muscles give the hand great flexibility and allow it to safely handle fragile objects. The fingertips are so sensitive that they can pick up a coin from a flat surface.

The ability to walk can allow an intelligent machine to adjust its position in its environment. Walking on two legs is something like a continuous, controlled fall that is avoided by carefully timing steps. People do it without thinking about it, but it is a challenge for machines. The engineers of Honda Research Institute of Japan developed a small robot that can walk, climb steps, open a door, pick up a phone, carry a tray, and play soccer. It is named ASIMO, which stands for Advanced Step in Innovative Mobility. ASIMO is 4 feet (1.2m) high and weighs about 115 pounds (52kg). It can walk backwards, sideways, and on a wide variety of surfaces at speeds up to a little over 1 mile per hour (1.6kmh). It is able to do this, because it has twenty-six joints that move in twenty-six different directions. This takes a lot of computing power, and ASIMO carries its own computer in a pack on its back. It is equipped with a gyroscope and speed sensor, so it can maintain its balance. It also has artificial visual perception in the form of three cameras, two in its head and one at its waist. ASIMO's nickel-zinc battery provides enough power for it to operate for about twenty-five minutes. ASIMO was created to assist people, especially those lacking full mobility.

Animal Moves

Not all robots walk on two legs. For some jobs, animal movement is the best solution. Scientists have built robotic fish that swim in the ocean to study pollution and robotic birds

A representative from the International Rescue System Institute demonstrates Souryu, a snake-like robot that is used to search through rubble for victims of earthquakes and other disasters.

that may one day be used to search collapsed buildings. Because of their ability to fly, robotic birds could land near tiny openings in unstable rubble. Their small size would allow them to enter and search inside for larger openings and trapped survivors. A robot sensor called DASH (dynamic autonomous sprawled hexapod) can cling to a wall or ceiling. DASH is cheap and versatile. Dozens of them could be placed on structures like bridges to monitor safety. To develop a wall-climbing robot, DASH's creators studied the foot structure of the gecko. Graduate student Paul Birkmeyer explains, "Running up a wall feels very different than running over a flat surface, and studies on cockroaches and geckos show they use very different foot motions for climbing and running."[21]

A body plan that has inspired the design of many small robots is that of the snake. The long flexible shape of a snake enables it to slide its body through small spaces, such as cracks and crevices, and over uneven surfaces. These traits have inspired engineers at the NASA Ames Research Center in California to develop a robot that is made up of multiple, small independent units connected in a flexible line. This style of robot has many advantages. It is lightweight, which is critical on a spacecraft. It is also easy to repair, because it is made with easily replaceable units called modules. Other benefits are that the snakebot can crawl from a spacecraft lander without a ramp. The flexible snake shape is also excellent for search and rescue. Souryu is a remote-controlled robot designed by professor Shigeo Hirose (1947–) of the Tokyo Institute of Technology in Japan. It can bend or roll to move through rubble, and it is equipped with a camera and microphone to search for victims.

The multilegged spider is the inspiration for the Comet II built by professor Kenzo Nonami. The 12-foot-long (3.7m) robot is an excellent example of an AI system designed to

BITS & BYTES

6,000

Number of computers in the world's largest working computer grid, the Large Hadron Collider Computing Grid (LCG). The system is spread over seventy-eight international locations.

The Robot Hall of Fame

Carnegie Mellon University in Pittsburgh, Pennsylvania, is home to the Robot Hall of Fame. The hall of fame honors robots that represent achievements in robotics technology and contributions to human endeavors. Robots may be nominated on the hall of fame's website by experts and by the general public. The hall of fame recognizes two categories of robots: robots from science and robots from science fiction. The robots from science are autonomous. They have each served a useful purpose in such fields as industry, science, education, or entertainment and have proven skills that support that purpose. The robots from science fiction are widely known from literature or film and have played an important role in shaping public opinion about robots.

Some Robot Hall of Fame Robots from Science

Sony AIBO. AIBO (Artificial Intelligence BOt) is a four-legged entertainment robot made available to the public between 1998 and 2006. AIBO could understand up to 100 voice commands.

SCARA (industrial robot arm). The SCARA (Selective Compliance Assembly Robot Arm) was first used on commercial assembly lines in 1981. Used to assemble products, the arm is fast and precise.

Shakey. Shaky was the first mobile robot that was able to complete a command without step-by-step directions. It was also capable of changing its behavior to adapt to unplanned barriers.

ASIMO. ASIMO (Advanced Step in Innovative Mobility) is the first robot to walk over and around obstacles much like humans do. ASIMO's talents include the ability to recognize facial expressions and gestures.

Sojourner (Mars rover). In 1997 Sojourner was the first robot to explore the surface of another planet. It analyzed rocks, soil, wind and temperature, and sent information and images to earth.

protect human life. It is designed to find land mines in war zones around the world. Such mines kill or injure as many as two thousand people every month. The robot walks on six sturdy metal legs. It uses a metal detector and radar unit to find mines and sprays paint on the ground to mark the spot.

AI at Work

Robots are a way for computers to interact with the physical world. They carry out AI programs designed to

Unimate (industrial robot arm). In 1961 Unimate joined the assembly line at a General Motors automotive plant. It performed tasks such as welding.

NavLab 5 (autonomous vehicles). NavLab 5 was a vehicle equipped with computers and sensors that enabled it to steer itself. In 1995 scientists drove across the United States with NavLab steering and the human passengers operating the brake and accelerator.

Some Robot Hall of Fame Robots from Science Fiction

David (*A. I. Artificial Intelligence*, 2001). David was the main character in director Steven Spielberg's film, *A. I. Artificial Intelligence*. An android that looked like a ten year-old boy, David was abandoned by his human parent.

Gort (*The Day the Earth Stood Still*, 1951). The movie classic, *The Day the Earth Stood Still*, featured a huge metallic robot named Gort. The robot guarded a humanoid space traveler named Klaatu.

Lieutenant Commander Data (*Star Trek: The Next Generation* television series, 1987–1994). Data was the chief operations officer of the USS Starship Enterprise. He was an android and beloved member of the starship crew.

C-3PO (*Star Wars* series, 1977–2005). A protocol droid able to speak six million binary languages, C-3PO was helpful in saving humanity from the evil emperor in the classic Star Wars film series.

R2-D2 (*Star Wars* series, 1977–2005). A small robot on wheels, R2-D2 communicated through chirps and whistles. Paired with C-3PO, R2-D2 bravely battled the evil emperor in the *Star Wars* series.

HAL 9000 (*2001: A Space Odyssey*, 1968). HAL 9000 (Heuristically programmed ALgorithmic computer) was the central computer that ran the systems of spaceship Discovery in *2001: A Space Odyssey*, directed by Stanley Kubrick.

Robby (*Forbidden Planet*, 1956). Robby was one of the first film robots. Robby was built on Planet Altair IV by Dr. Edward Morbius from plans left in an alien computer system.

benefit humans in the workplace and at home. Robots are generally cost-effective and reliable and are often employed in work that is known as 4D: dangerous, dirty, dull, or dumb. Industrial robots labor in factories around the world. An industrial robot must be, among other things, automatically controlled and reprogrammable. It can be either fixed in place or mobile. Most are used to move heavy or toxic materials or to perform such repetitive jobs as spot welding and painting. There are certain advantages to using robots instead of humans in the workplace. They are faster and more precise. They can work twenty-four hours a day, seven days a week. And robots do not get bored or tired, and they can work almost anywhere.

It may seem unlikely to find robots in a hay field, but an agricultural hay harvester named Demeter may soon be doing much of the labor on large commercial farms. The robotic machine is programmed to automatically steer, drive, and control the harvester, while the operator is in the cab. It may also be programmed to use GPS to map a field and repeat the path so that one operator can remotely control several harvesters. A fully autonomous harvester is equipped with vision perception, so that it can harvest a field with no human supervision.

A service robot does jobs that are useful to the well-being of humans. One type of service robot is the personal robot. Personal robots include those that assist people with disabilities, those that serve as a companions, and those that serve as pets. One example of a pet robot is Pleo, a baby *Camarasaurus* that was created for people who wanted a pet dinosaur. Pleo is interactive. It has a camera-based vision system, microphones, a sensor that can detect a beat so it can dance to music, and an array of touch sensors. The domestic robot is another type of service robot, and there is a wide range of them that do everything from cleaning a cat's litterbox to mowing the lawn. The Roomba is a well-known example of a housekeeping robot. Its only duty is to vacuum floors and carpets. It looks like a beetle and it moves around in a predetermined area. Roomba has a large contact-sensing bumper that prevents it from bumping into walls and furniture.

Professor Daniel T. Barry (1953–) notes that these types of systems are becoming more common. Barry has a robot at home that can take a pizza from the delivery person, pay for it, and carry it into the kitchen. "You have the robot say, 'Take the 20 and leave the pizza on top of me.'" Barry says, "I get the pizza about a third of the time."[22]

Robot Explorers

Every day thousands of robots employing expert systems, artificial senses, natural language processing, and other elements of AI work side by side with people. Telerobotics is the area of AI concerned with the practical use of robots. AI in telerobotic form is regularly used in exploration that is too expensive or too dangerous for humans. The remotely operated vehicle (ROV) and the remote manipulator system (RMS) are designed for space exploration. ROVs may be unmanned spacecraft landers that land on extraterrestrial bodies or rovers that can move over the surface. *Sojourner* was the first rover to explore another planet. It was part of the mission of *Pathfinder*, a spacecraft sent to Mars on December 4, 1996. *Sojourner* analyzed Martian rocks and soil and transmitted over five hundred photographs to Earth. The six-wheeled rover is about 2 feet long (.61m), 1.5 feet wide (.46m), and about 1 foot (.30m) tall, and it weighed about 24 pounds (10.9kg). Like most rovers, *Sojourner* was semiautonomous, and it could be remotely controlled from Earth.

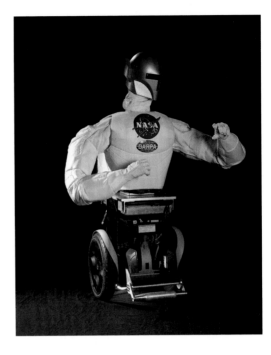

NASA has created a series of Robonauts, mechanical astronauts that may enable aspects of space exploration that is too dangerous for humans to conduct.

Because the human body is too fragile for the harsh temperatures and radiation in space, NASA designed a series of robonauts that mimic the actions of a human. These AI-based robotic astronauts are operated by human astronauts within a spacecraft. The robonauts have two color-video cameras mounted in the headpiece. The arms are equipped with more than 150 sensors for maximum input, and the five-digit hands can use tools designed for humans. What the robonauts do not have, however, is a pair of legs—one version of the robot has been designed with a single leg and another has a pair of wheels.

It is not necessary to travel into space to explore a harsh, exotic region. The Arctic Ocean is also an extremely hostile environment for humans. In 1998, as part of the Jeremy Project, a partnership between NASA (National Aeronautics and Space Administration) and Santa Clara University in California, researchers deployed a small submersible telerobot into the freezing Arctic water. Carrying sensors and control mechanisms, the telepresence remotely operated vehicle (TROV) explored two whaling ships that sank in the late 1800s. A power cable connected the robot and the research vessel, where the scientists monitored the TROV. The machine gathered valuable information, while the human operators were safely aboard their ship, the *Polar Star*.

Hazardous Duty

One of the world's most dangerous jobs is that of bomb disposal. When a job is so hazardous that a human cannot be on the site, using a telerobot to do the job is often the best option. Rather than following a programmed set of instructions, a bomb disposal telerobot is controlled from a safe distance by a human operator. The British military employs a bomb disposal robot that weighs 14 pounds (6.4kg) and fits into a backpack. Known as the Dragon Runner, it has four cameras and is operated by a handheld controller. The robot is fitted with a manipulator arm that can dig around and lift items that weigh up to 10 pounds (4.5kg). It can also place small explosive charges that disable suspicious objects.

Many robotic systems are used in the military forces of many countries including the United States. Unmanned military ground vehicles (UGV) include a wide range of telerobots, such as minesweepers, bomb disposal units, and units that gather information. MIDARS is a four-wheeled robot guard that is designed to patrol a military base. Equipped with cameras and radar, it can search for intruders and alert a human operator in case of a threat or

To Protect and Serve

The 1987 film *RoboCop* is set in an American city plagued by crime. When a police officer is killed in the line of duty, he is re-created as a cyborg. Three prime directives are part of his programming: serve the public trust, protect the innocent, and uphold the law. He is equipped with an array of weapons and tools for fighting crime, including an outer suit, or exoskeleton, that repels bullets and survives intense heat and flames.

The law enforcement officer of the future may have something in common with RoboCop: a powerful and protective exoskeleton. Using nanotechnology, Australian researchers at the University of Sydney have developed a material that causes bullets to bounce off of it. In Japan, Professor Shigeki Toyama of the Tokyo University of Agriculture and Technology has created a suit with eight electric motors that amplify the strength of the wearer's arms and legs, and sensors that respond to commands through a voice-recognition system. The U.S. Army is also using robotics to expand human capabilities with a 150-pound (kg) suit that senses and amplifies the wearer's strength. In the future the technology will be available for police and firefighters.

A software engineer tests a robotic suit crafted for the U.S. Army that would increase a soldier's strength and endurance.

Technologies that exist or are in development for the exoskeleton of the future include:

- Color-shifting nanotechnology fabric to enable the wearer to blend into the background.
- Instant computer voice translator to enable wearer to speak in any language.
- Helmet with incoming tactical data projected on inside of visor.
- Nano-muscle fibers in suit to enhance wearer's muscle strength.

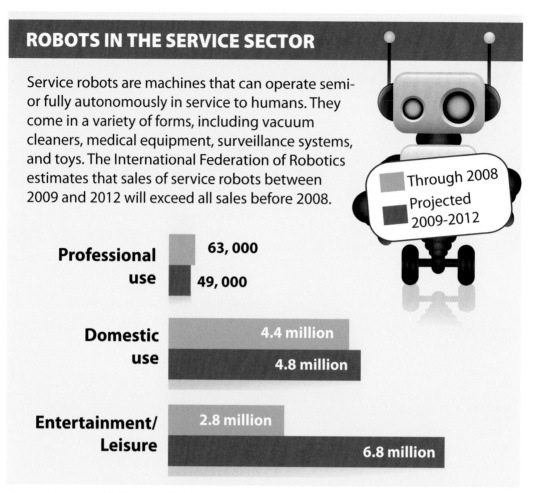

ROBOTS IN THE SERVICE SECTOR

Service robots are machines that can operate semi- or fully autonomously in service to humans. They come in a variety of forms, including vacuum cleaners, medical equipment, surveillance systems, and toys. The International Federation of Robotics estimates that sales of service robots between 2009 and 2012 will exceed all sales before 2008.

Through 2008
Projected 2009-2012

Professional use
63,000
49,000

Domestic use
4.4 million
4.8 million

Entertainment/ Leisure
2.8 million
6.8 million

Source: International Federation of Robotics. "Service Robot Statistics." www.ifr.org/service-robots/statistics/

an emergency. The Predator may be one of the best-known unmanned vehicles. It is an aircraft, also called a drone. It can search terrain, take photographs, and fire on targets from the air.

Healing Humans

Robots are not only being employed to protect humans, but also to heal them. AI-based robotic surgical systems are used in medical centers in dozens of countries around the world to assist as doctors do surgery. Surgeries require as many as a dozen nurses and doctors in the operating room. Robotic systems can reduce that number and still improve the safety and success of surgeries. Someday AI-based robots may operate without having a human surgeon directly involved.

In July 2000 the da Vinci Surgical System became the first robotic system allowed in U.S. operating rooms. It is used in laparoscopic, or minimally invasive surgery (MIS). The surgeon makes a small opening in the patient's body and inserts a tiny laparoscope, a tool that includes a camera, a knife, and the ability to provide suction and fluid spray. Images taken by the camera appear on a large screen in the operating room. In a traditional heart surgery, a 12-inch (30cm) cut is made in the patient's chest. With the da Vinci

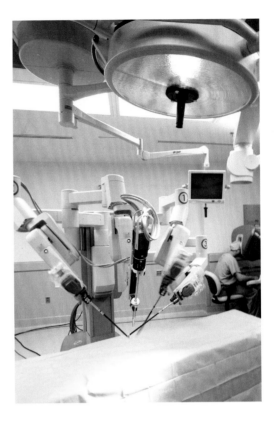

system, the surgeon makes several smaller incisions, so the patient experiences less pain and bleeding, which means a faster recovery. The da Vinci Surgical System is a telesurgical device, meaning a human surgeon guides the motions of the robotic device. In 2010 surgeons at Canada's McGill University Health Centre performed the first all-robotic surgery on a living patient. Doctors controlled the da Vinci system, but no part of the procedure was done by human hands. Even the anesthesia was delivered by a robot named McSleepy. In the future, doctors might be able to use similar robotic tools to perform long-distance surgery on a patient many miles away.

A hospital operating room is equipped with a Da Vinci Surgical System, which is controlled remotely by a surgeon working at a computer console.

The Path Ahead

Researchers face several challenges when creating robots with varying degrees of AI. One challenge is that robotics

The Three Laws

According to the *Oxford English Dictionary*, the first use of the term *robotics* was by science-fiction author Isaac Asimov (1920–1992). It appears in his short story *Liar!* published in 1941. Another Asimov story about robots, titled *Runaround* and published in 1941, includes three laws of robotics, which many AI researchers agree are a good framework as robots play a larger role in society. The laws prevent robots from harming or disobeying humans.

Asimov's Three Laws of Robotics

1. A robot may not injure a human, or, through inaction, allow a human being to come to harm.
2. A robot must obey the orders it is given by human beings except where such orders would conflict with the First Law.
3. A robot must protect its own existence as long as such protection does not conflict with the First or Second Law.[1]

After Asimov's laws were published, other authors added to the list. In *Icarus's Way*, published in 1974, Bulgarian writer, Lyuben Dilov added a fourth law: "A robot must establish its identity as a robot in all cases."[2] In a novel titled *The Fifth Law* another Bulgarian writer, Nikola Kesarovski, added that a robot must know it is a robot.

1. Isaac Asimov. "Runaround." *Astounding Science-Fiction*, March 1942, pp. 94–103
2. "Ethics of Robot Behavior." IEEE Global History Network, March 3, 2009. www.ieeeghn.org/wiki/index.php/Ethics_of_Robot_Behaviour.

companies do not have a standard operating software that allows different programs to be used with a variety of machines. Complex robots are also expensive to produce, and although many advances have been made, no robot has ever passed the Turing Test. Nonetheless, each accomplishment brings the field closer to developing a robot with true intelligence.

In 2007, writer Robin Henig noted,

Robots are not the docile companions of our collective dreams, robots designed to flawlessly serve our dinners, fold our clothes and do the dull or dangerous jobs that we don't want to do. Nor are they the villains of our collective nightmares. . . . They are, instead, hunks of metal tethered to computers, which need their human designers to get them going and to smooth the hiccups along the way.[23]

CHAPTER **4**

The Future of Artificial Intelligence

S ince the 1960s, artificial intelligence (AI) in the form of computer programs and robotics has brought about many changes in the world. Some people predict that it will not be long before robots will be caring for elderly humans and that people will regularly travel by means of virtual reality suits— full body suits with wireless electrodes that detect the user's movements and goggles that create a visual environment. Researchers predict the development of autonomous robots that are able to rebuild or even reproduce themselves and tiny robots no bigger than a single cell. Machines may incorporate more human traits, such as emotion and creativity, and the future may hold robotically enhanced humans and even a blend of human and machine intelligence.

AI and Human Emotion

As of the early twenty-first century, a strong human-machine relationship already exists in society. Since the introduction of computers, video games, the Internet, and smartphones, some people spend more hours each day with machines than with other humans. A user can even create a chatbot, an artificial personality designed to engage in a casual online conversation.

When it comes to simulating human decision making, however, a machine's inability to experience emotion may be a drawback. In 1996 author Rosalind W. Picard pointed out, "The inability of today's computers to recognize, express, and have emotions severely limits their ability to act intelligently and interact naturally with us."[24] Some researchers believe that thought and emotion are linked and humans make better decisions when they are emotionally involved. For example, fear can prevent a person from making a dangerous choice, and love motivates a parent to protect his or her child.

Kismet, a robot created at the Massachusetts Institute of Technology, is programmed to interact with humans by processing sensory inputs and making facial expressions.

Thanks to breakthroughs in AI, such as software that enables robots to recognize human emotions based on facial expressions, tone of voice, and gestures, scientists are now creating computers and robots that can identify and respond to a human user's feelings. The next step will be creating a machine that is capable of experiencing and expressing human emotion.

Some researchers are using emotional-logic software to create more instinctive interactions between humans and robots. Scientists at Utrecht University in the Netherlands have built a robotic cat programmed with a set of logical rules for emotions. They believe that this will enable a human to interact more naturally with the machine, called iCAT. Using its eyebrows, eyelids, mouth, and head position, the robot displays facial expressions. Mehdi Dastani, an artificial-intelligence researcher at the university says, "We don't really believe that computers can have emotions, but we see that emotions have a certain function in human practical reasoning."[25] He adds that by giving intelligent machines emotions, they might develop humanlike reasoning and "make rational decision-making processes more realistic and much more computable."[26]

Researchers hope that future robots will not only be able to imitate emotions, but also to experience them. Two robots—eMo, introduced in 2003 and Kismet, introduced in 1999—exhibit the efforts being made in this direction. Although it is simply a mechanical head, eMo greets visitors at Thinktank, a science museum in Birmingham, England. It has a computer-controlled face with digital cameras for eyes and lips that move. The robot interacts with guests who enter the gallery. Even though eMo does not experience feelings, it can reflect a range of human expressions, including happiness, surprise, sadness, and anger.

Kismet, a robot from the Massachusetts Institute of Technology in Massachusetts, is equipped with visual, auditory, and other sensory inputs. It can speak, use facial expressions, and change the direction of its eyes and the tilt of its head. When a human interacts with Kismet, the robot turns its gaze toward the person and appears to listen. Kismet displays an assortment of facial expressions. It can perk up its ears to show that it is interested or fold them back to show anger or annoyance. The lips are able to form a smile or a frown, and the eyebrows raise, lower, slant, and furrow to show confusion. Kismet also winks and blinks.

The robot uses certain body movements to communicate. If a person is too close, the robot moves its head back as people do when someone invades their personal space. Kismet has other social skills, too. For example, it looks at the person who is speaking, appears to listen attentively, and takes turns in conversation. The robot uses visual clues to know when to do what. Perhaps the most surprising thing is how easily Kismet brings out emotional reactions from its visitors who smile, move closer, or back away in response to the robot's expressions.

If robots had additional capabilities in understanding and expressing emotions, their usefulness could expand into new areas in which human interaction is important. For example, a future use for emotional robots could be in patient therapy. Supporters of the idea say that robot therapy would be similar to animal assisted therapy, better known as pet therapy, in which patients benefit by interacting with friendly dogs or other animals to reduce anxiety, increase physical movement, and more. In a 2004 report from Japan, researchers found that during robot therapy sessions some hospital patients talked and touched the robot more than they touched a human therapist. Their reactions were similar to that of patients who interacted with therapy animals and even stuffed animals. In some cases, a therapy robot might be a better choice than a therapy animal, because it can be programmed to perform special tasks for patients, such as reminding them to take their medicine.

Robots may also become welcomed as caregivers in the United States, since approximately 77 million Americans are expected to retire between 2011 and 2041, and many will require personal care. This is likely to put more of a

FIRST IMPRESSIONS

In a 2007 survey, conducted by members of the Swiss Federal Institute of Technology and the Ecole Polytechnique Fédérale de Lausanne (EPFL), participants responded negatively to the idea of domestic robots resembling living creatures.

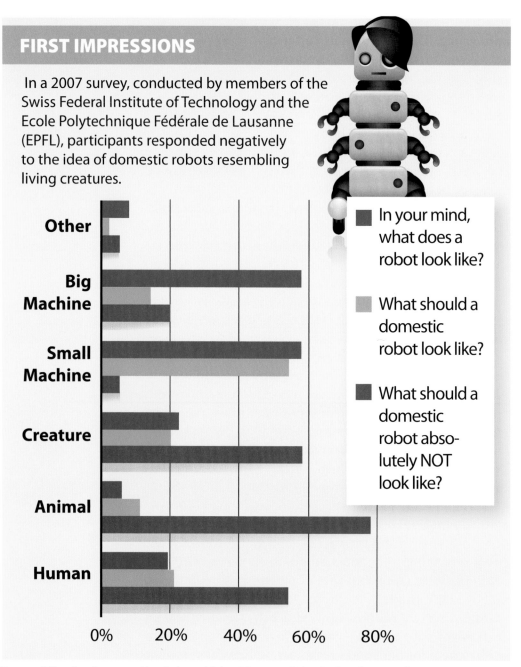

Legend:
- In your mind, what does a robot look like?
- What should a domestic robot look like?
- What should a domestic robot absolutely NOT look like?

Categories (top to bottom): Other, Big Machine, Small Machine, Creature, Animal, Human

X-axis: 0%, 20%, 40%, 60%, 80%

Source: Céline Ray, Francesco Mondada, and Roland Siegwart. "What Do People Expect from Robots?" http://infoscience.epfl.ch/record/125291/files/iros08_ray_final-10.pdf?version=1.

strain on health-care providers as well as on the economy of the United States. Assistance robots could prove to be an economical way to improve the daily life of the elderly as well as people with disabilities because they can work longer hours than humans at a lower per patient cost, and they may enable many patients to continue to live at home. The uBot-5 is a personal-care robot that can provide many patient services. It can remind a person to take medication and call 911. The uBot-5 has a webcam, a microphone, and a touch-sensitive LCD display that acts as an interface for contact with the outside world. Family members and doctors can access the unit to check on the patient through an Internet connection. With an assistance robot nearby, the elderly could remain independent and stay in their own homes instead of moving to a retirement facility or moving in with family. Advances in robotics may produce robot caregivers that can help with shopping, housework, personal cleanliness, and even emergencies.

Synthetic Imagination

Incorporating aspects of positive human emotions into AI programming could be an important step toward the development of strong AI. Another positive human trait is creativity. Like some emotions, creativity is hard to define. Many people have natural artistic talent for painting, poetry, or playing music. A branch of AI research, called computational creativity, is focused on the study of this important element of human intelligence. A goal for the future is to develop AI that can produce creative work that is original, unique, and inventive.

There have been several attempts to build creative computers. One of these is AARON, a painting program that generates both abstract and lifelike art. Abstract artist and computer programmer Harold Cohen developed the program and a corresponding database about form, color theory, and composition. At first, AARON produced only simple line sketches. As Cohen expanded the program with information about shapes, AARON

Harold Cohen oversees a painting created by AARON, a program he developed that is able to produce both abstract and lifelike art.

began to create pictures of humans in recognizable environments. AARON now produces color illustrations that show what some artists say is a certain amount of skill and imagination.

Another creative intelligence project was led by Philip Johnson-Laird, a psychologist at Princeton University in New Jersey. He became interested in machine creativity while he was studying memory in jazz musicians. Using a rule-based AI programming language, he devised a program that improvises modern jazz with chord sequences and melodies.

The purpose of teaching computers to think creatively is not just to produce great visual art or great musical compositions. Because creative thinking includes an element of randomness, or chance, it could lead to breakthroughs

Association for the Advancement of Artificial Intelligence

The Association for the Advancement of Artificial Intelligence (AAAI) is an international scientific organization dedicated to advancing the understanding of the mechanisms of artificial intelligence. It was founded in 1979 and is based in Menlo Park, California. Many of the most influential figures in AI research have served as the association's president. They include Allen Newell, a National Medal of Science recipient; Marvin Minsky, the cofounder of the Computer Science and Artificial Intelligence Laboratory at the Massachusetts Institute of Technology; and John McCarthy, who coined the term *artificial intelligence* for the 1956 Dartmouth Artificial Intelligence Conference.

One of the goals of AAAI is to improve the training of those who practice AI and help the general public understand developments in the field. The society sponsors meetings, conferences, and workshops. It publishes the *Journal of Artificial Intelligence Research* and *AI Magazine*, which includes articles on significant new research in the field of artificial intelligence. The association also maintains a website that offers information on a wide range of AI-related topics. The website also provides resources for students with tips for writing reports, researching projects, and giving talks.

in other areas. In *A Proposal for the Dartmouth Summer Research Project on Artificial Intelligence*, the formal proposal for the Dartmouth Artificial Intelligence Conference of 1956, researchers note, "The educated guess or the hunch include controlled randomness in otherwise orderly thinking."[27] If computational creativity is successful, then many great discoveries of the future may be based on computer hunches.

Artificial Worlds

The field of virtual reality (VR) is a modern technology that benefits from the development of computer creativity. VR enables users to interact with computer-simulated

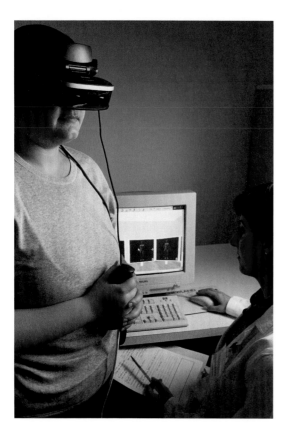

A patient wears a headset as part of a virtual reality system used for behavioral therapy, one of many practical applications of the technology.

environments. The simplest form of VR is an interactive image on a personal computer. Computer users are placed into the virtual environment in a variety of ways, from a monitor to a head-mounted display or a glove. The user controls the actions of the image using a keyboard or mouse. More complex systems involve wrap-around display screens and special gloves and goggles, or actual rooms with wearable computers.

There are different definitions for a true VR experience, but in general it should include three-dimensional images; a method for tracking a user's hand, head, and eye movements; and a way to adjust the images that the user sees. Virtual reality may incorporate AI to create elements of the environment that are not controlled by the user.

A practical use of a VR system is in operation at Brown University in Rhode Island to help people who have fears and phobias. For example, a person who is afraid of flying in airplanes wears a headset, sits in an airline seat, and experiences a flight in a controlled environment. This allows a mental health professional to monitor and discuss the fearful person's experience as it happens. Supporters of virtual reality claim that in the future VR will be an important part of education.

Michael Donfrancesco of InterSense, a company that produces VR products, suggests that VR will soon be available on the Internet and in television studios to create virtual sets or backgrounds. He says, "We will soon be immersed inside the Internet, interacting with it virtually in three dimensions. We may all wear personal headsets that allow us to walk through scenes we now see in two dimensions on our computer monitors."[28] In their book, *Virtual Marketing: Through the New Looking Glass*, Ken Pimental and Kevin Teixeira proposed that, "within one hundred years virtual reality could become a semi-invisible service in society, like telephones, light switches, books, and television—a tool for communication, work, and pleasure that we use without thinking about it."[29]

Someday, every home may have its own virtual reality system and change the way people live. Author Ramesh Jain explains, "You might experience your friend's wedding in India, seeing what is happening, feeling the warm, humid air of the wedding hall, listening to conversations and the wedding music, and enjoying the taste and aroma of the food being served. You might experience all that and more while sitting at home."[30] Still, the technology may have a downside. Some researchers think that regular use of VR systems might have an effect on brain function. VR could change the way that people view the real world and cause them to withdraw into a world of imagination. The hope is that VR will actually help to expand the world by giving people the opportunity to experience places they might never go otherwise.

Minibots

While areas of AI research, such as those that deal with VR, are focusing on expanding the scope of new technology, others are trying to make AI innovations physically smaller. Some researchers think the future could include clouds of insect-size autonomous robots buzzing around and doing jobs such as cleaning pipes and drains, finding lost objects, and even spying. Scientists, inspired by colonies of ants and bees, are developing minibots that work in swarms. Each robot is small and simple, but a set of hundreds or even thousands of them work together as a single system with complex behaviors. For example, a swarm could be given the task of searching a collapsed building. It would first map the area and then search the

An illustration imagines how a medical nanobot, which would measure about one-billionth of a meter, would attack bacteria or perform surgery at a cellular level.

building. The robots could use their sensors to support firefighters or police officers by gathering information in a building that is on fire or filled with smoke, or in a building where a crime is in progress. Among the many benefits of a swarm is its reliability. If a single large robot fails on a mission, then that mission is over. If a few members of a swarm fail, the others take over. This could make minibots a good choice for space missions, where defective robots cannot be easily repaired.

The future of medicine may include intelligent robots smaller than the eye can see. Nanorobotics is a technology that exists only as an idea. It is the science of creating robotic

Upgrade: Nanobots and Microbots

Some people predict that by 2030 nanobots the size of blood cells will commonly help keep humans healthy. Scientists at the Massachusetts Institute of Technology are working on microscopic devices that can locate and destroy cancer cells in the bloodstream. Nanobots could eventually be used to repair DNA errors and destroy toxins and disease-causing agents.

A prototype for a system called OctoMag, created at the Institute of Robotics and Intelligent Systems in Zurich, Switzerland, is designed to eliminate blood clots in the human eye. OctoMag is made up of a field of tightly coiled, 5-DOF (five-degree-of-freedom) magnets. The procedure is simple. The surgeon injects a half-millimeter long microbot into the patient's nose then uses the magnets to guide the minirobot through the small vessels of the eye to reach and destroy the clot.

In the opinion of author and inventor Raymond Kurzweil, nanobots may even be used for entertainment. He suggests that a person could travel the world virtually by injecting tiny nanobots into the brain. The nanobots would be programmed to stimulate human neurons and convince the brain that the person is traveling. The tour could be complete with sights, sounds, and smells. Kurzweil admits that such technology is far in the future and that it would not be risk free. A nanobot could stimulate the wrong part of the brain and create a nightmare or even a seizure.

machines or robots about the size of a nanometer, or one-billionth of a meter. That means that nanobots, also called nanites, would be much smaller than the smallest bacterium. These tiny robots could possibly be used to perform surgery at the level of the cell. Decades from now intelligent nano-robots might be routinely used to examine the human body from the inside.

The Shape of Things to Come

Nanobots are one form that AI of the future might take. Another is the half-human, half-machine structure of the cyborg. A cyborg is a blend of natural and artificial parts, where the mechanical parts enhance or support the body's

Professor Kevin Warwick holds a microchip like the one implanted in his left arm in 1998 and again in 2002, allowing him to connect his body to a wireless computer network.

natural systems. Given this definition, cyborgs already exist in the twenty-first century. They are people who have a pacemaker attached to the heart or have a hearing aid implanted in the ear.

Kevin Warwick (1954–), professor of cybernetics at the University of Reading in Great Britain, experimented with the idea of adding AI to his body in 1998 and again in 2002. In 1998 he had a tiny silcon chip transponder implanted in his left arm. The chip transmitted a signal to a computer network that Warwick used to operate doors, lights, and other computers from a distance without having to use a remote control device. The computer network was able to recognize the origin of the unique signal so Warwick could be tracked no matter where he was on the campus. It has been suggested that if several people had similar chips, they could possibly transmit signals to each other over the Internet. In 2002 Warwick had an electrode array surgically implanted into the nerve fibers of his left arm. This array allowed him to remotely operate an electric wheelchair and an intelligent artificial hand. Bionic implants are another place where advanced AI may lead to breakthroughs. These implants are electromechanical replacement parts for damaged natural limbs or organs. Bionic implants use AI to mimic the function of the natural body part and can help preserve a person's quality of life. In the near future, brain implants might help to restore eyesight for a blind person or limb function for someone who is paralyzed.

Advanced AI software could also improve brain-computer interface (BCI) technology. BCI provides a direct path of communication from the brain to an external device. With BCI, a person could perform tasks, such as operating a computer, without having to move. In the future, this technology could also have recreational applications.

Radio-frequency identification (RFID) is a nonmedical cyborg function in which an information chip or tag is inserted under a person's skin. The technology is already being used with animals. Pet owners "microchip" their pets with a rice-sized chip that contains the owner's contact information. Veterinarians insert the chip just under the pet's skin. Chips for people could contain a wide range of information, such as medical and financial details and insurance data. AI systems could assist with mining this data for a variety of useful purposes. Some people oppose this idea because the chip could be used to track individuals, and it could lead to a loss of privacy.

Creating Cyborgs

In the future, cyborg insects, such as dragonflies, moths, and bees, may become part of military organizations. In 2009 researchers demonstrated the first wireless flying-insect cyborg, and engineers at the University of California at Berkeley introduced a design for a remote-controlled cyborg flower beetle. The insects transmit data from sensors implanted during the pupal stage of their development. The tiny cyborgs may do important work in the future. Jack Judy, manager of the cyborg insect program says, "The intimate control of insects with embedded microsystems will enable insect cyborgs, which could carry one or more sensors, such as a microphone or a gas sensor, to relay back information gathered from the target destination."[31] Researchers are also considering the value of implanting certain ocean life, such as sharks, with AI systems. The implants could one day track ship movements and detect underwater explosives.

An illustration depicts a cyborg fly. Researchers are envisioning ways that flying insect robots could be useful in military operations and intelligence-gathering activities.

Cyborg technology may also be used someday to enhance healthy humans beyond their natural abilities. According to philosopher Max More,

> the neuron is a biochemical machine. We should therefore be able to replace or repair damaged neural tissue with implants and supplement biological neurons with synthetic neurons while retaining the same functions. We should be able to add memory, processing power, and new abilities by doing so. In principle, we could replace all our neurons until we had an entirely synthetic or prosthetic brain.[32]

Author and inventor Raymond Kurzweil (1948–) agrees. He says, "We will transcend all of the limitations of our biology. That is what it means to be human, to extend who we are."[33]

This idea is popular among some people who suggest that humans need to involve intelligent machines in the human evolutionary process. This has led to a movement called transhumanism, which endorses the use of implants and other technologies to enhance human beings. Transhumanism has been described by Francis Fukuyama, professor of international political economy at Johns Hopkins School of Advanced International Studies, as the world's most dangerous idea that wants "nothing less than to liberate the human race from its biological constraints."[34] Others call it daring and imaginative. It is a movement that promotes technologies, such as AI. Supporters claim that AI can help to create a future free of disease and even aging, in part by blending natural and machine intelligence.

MSRS and EATR

Modular self-reconfiguring robotic systems (MSRS) are robots that can change their own shape by rearranging the way their parts are connected. They may do this to adapt to a change in the environment or in a job or to repair damage. MSRS robots are made up of easily changed parts, or modules, that can be assembled in a variety of ways. For example, a robot could use a snake-like movement to get through a

A Great Deal

Since 1960 computers have become faster, smaller, cheaper, and easier to use. These improvements accelerated from 1990 to 2010. In fact, according to computer science teacher Roderick Hames in 2009, "had the automobile developed at a pace equal to that of the computer during the past twenty years, today a Rolls Royce would cost less than $3.00, get 3 million miles to the gallon, deliver enough power to drive the ship Queen Elizabeth II, and six of them would fit on the head of a pin!"

Roderick Hames. "The Computer Emerges!" *Computer Daily News* 1, no. 1 (Spring 2009). www.crews.org/curriculum/ex/compsci/articles/history.htm.

narrow pipe, then assume the shape of a wheel in order to roll quickly over flat terrain, and then become a many-legged form to crawl over a rocky landscape. Each module may contain a power supply as well as sensors, processors, memory, and other components. Engineers are designing some modules to automatically connect and disconnect themselves to and from each other. Modules may even be interchangeable between robots. The machines would also be able to replace faulty parts or repair themselves without the help of a human operator, possibly even building entirely new robots from a bucket of modules.

There are other advantages to the MSRS. It would be cheaper to produce because most of the modules would be alike so they could be mass-produced. The adaptable system would be ideal for space travel, since it would reduce the amount of equipment that needs to be transported.

Future robotic vehicles may also run on a wide range of substances and be able to find their own fuel. The Energetically Autonomous Tactical Robot (EATR) is an unmanned robotic vehicle used for transporting weapons and other materials. It is in development by the Defense Advanced Research Projects Agency (DARPA) for the U.S. military. The EATR runs on biofuel such as plants.

It senses when it needs to be refueled, and it can forage for plants. It also runs on gasoline, coal, cooking oil, and solarenergy.

What Is Next?

Advancements in AI, robotics, medicine, and genetics continue to result in remarkable developments. In early 2010, Synthetic Genomics, a biotech company, announced that it had created a synthetic bacterial genome, opening up the possibility of the development of artificial life. A genome is the complete set of instructions for building and maintaining a living organism.

The company's researchers reported that they used the synthetic genome to take over a living cell, creating a synthetic cell. Scientist J. Craig Venter, cofounder, chairman, and chief executive officer of Synthetic Genomics, claims that the technology could lead the way to creating cells from scratch. He explains that the converted cell is the "the first self-replicating species we've had on the planet whose parent is a computer."[35]

CHAPTER 5

The Ethics of Artificial Intelligence

Sometimes the future of artificial intelligence (AI) seems like science fiction. It is possible that sometime during the twenty-first century, machine intelligence will far exceed human intelligence. Intelligent machines may also develop the ability to share their knowledge and even teach each other. Some researchers have suggested that human minds could eventually be uploaded as software, creating a human-machine interface. If such developments take place, they will present many challenges. Will superhuman computers understand the difference between right and wrong? Will robots have rights or will they be considered property? Could the spread of machine intelligence lead to human job loss or loss of individual privacy? These questions will need to be addressed. In addition, freedom, free will, emotion, and many other concepts will have to be reevaluated, because they may not have the same meaning for humans, cyborgs, robots, and intelligent computers.

On the Silver Screen

Science-fiction writers have been exploring the ethical issues of AI for decades. Although the issues overlap, they may be loosely divided into three categories: How may beneficial forms of strong AI be integrated into society and what rights do they have? What does it mean to be human and at what point does AI cross the line to a true sapient, or intelligent being? Could a form of strong AI become a danger to humanity? These questions have been addressed in dozens of movies and quite a few television series. One of the most popular television series is *Star Trek: The Next Generation* (1987–1994). It features a character that is an android, or humanoid robot, named Lieutenant Commander Data. As a member of a space crew of humans, Data struggles to learn his place in human society. He has the ability to experience many things the same way humans do. In fact, he shows human qualities, including curiosity and loyalty. In the first few seasons of the series, the android has trouble understanding his human crewmates, because he has no emotions. Eventually his creator installs an emotion chip, and the android explores such feelings as sadness, sympathy, anger, and fear.

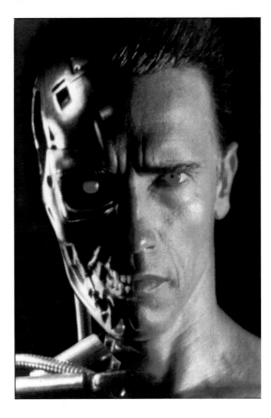

Arnold Schwarzenegger starred in the Terminator *movies as a murderous cyborg, one of several examples of how film and television have portrayed artificial intelligence at odds with humanity.*

The movie *Blade Runner* (1982) examines what it means to be human and poses the question of whether or not a form of strong AI might be considered a life form. It is based on the book, *Do Androids Dream of Electric Sheep?*, written by science-fiction author Philip K. Dick and published in 1968. It is about a man named Decker who hunts down artificially created humans called replicants. The replicants are used to do unpleasant work on space colonies and they are not allowed on Earth. When they defy that ban, blade runners like Decker are assigned to find and terminate them.

The *Terminator* film series (1984–) is about a society that has been taken over by a supercomputer system called Skynet. When the system becomes self-aware, it uses robots and cyborgs to enslave and humans, and eliminate millions. The bleak world portrayed in these films is unlikely to develop in reality, but many AI researchers agree that an ethical system for dealing with artificial life forms will be needed.

On Being Human

One of the main questions that many science-fiction writers ask is: What does it mean to be human? Some scientists define it as having consciousness and self-awareness. And some people believe that AI can achieve consciousness and self-awareness. Advances in computer hardware, software programming, and information storage are occurring rapidly. As of the early twenty-first century, computing speeds are approaching the computing power of the human brain. Gordon E. Moore (1929–), cofounder of the company Intel, created Moore's Law in a paper he wrote in 1965. Moore's Law states that the number of transistors on a computer chip doubles every two years. In the paper Moore notes that the number of components in integrated circuits doubled every year from their invention in 1958 until 1965 and he predicted that the trend would continue "for at least ten years."[36]

Moore's prediction turned out to be correct. Some people believe that this pace in technology may lead to a time when advances build on each other so quickly that they seem to take place almost instantly. One of the fastest present-day supercomputers is the IBM Blue Gene/P. It regularly operates at speeds of over a million billion operations per second. This computing power might eventually lead to the development of an AI system that has all of the elements of human intelligence, including language skills, a deep knowledge of the world, and the ability to think, feel, imagine, and create. Such a machine would probably understand experience and could possibly develop a form of artificial consciousness.

Moore's Law

In 1965, Intel co-founder Gordon Moore predicted ... of transistors on a piece of silicon would double ... years—an insight ... ed "Moore's Law." Hi ... held true ... istor sizes have ... growth ... s on a single ch ... Moore'... e electronics ... applies ... ompany. Who ... people to p ... unicate ha ... the company ... Moore's L

Intel Corp. cofounder Gordon E. Moore created Moore's Law in 1965, which accurately predicted the exponential growth of technology over the next decade and beyond.

Friendly Artificial Intelligence

Ryszard Michalski was a professor of computational sciences and one of the pioneers of machine learning, the ability of computers to improve their performance over time by making corrections based on previous results. He pointed out that machine minds are unknowable and therefore dangerous. This led to the development of Friendly Artificial Intelligence (FAI), computer systems that are designed to be sympathetic toward humans. Supporters of FAI suggest several ways to ensure that intelligent machines remain safe for humanity. Their goal is to design robots that are friendly toward humans because they want to be, not because they are forced to be. The following are elements that might be part of the programming of a human-friendly form of artificial intelligence.

1. An AI must be programmed to feel sympathy toward humans and all life, and act in the best interests of living things.
2. An AI must be programmed to pass on its value system to others of its kind.
3. An AI must be programmed to exhibit unselfish behavior and treat all living things with equal kindness.
4. An AI should be programmed to improve itself and all life, while respecting the choice of others not to improve themselves.

Some modern robots have already reached various levels of independence, such as being able to find power sources on their own, but none have attained artificial consciousness (AC) or synthetic consciousness. The ability to predict events and anticipate what will happen is an important element of AC. An artificially conscious machine should also be able to respond correctly to such events when they take place. To show that it has consciousness, a machine must demonstrate that it understands complex concepts, such as past, present, and future. It also has to demonstrate that it understands that it has a role in the events that are taking place.

The Turing Test is the best-known method for measuring machine intelligence, and it may help to identify artificial consciousness. Because the test depends on behavior, there is a small chance that a machine that has achieved consciousness could fail. In 2011 a new scale was developed. Called

Becoming an Artificial Intelligence Specialist

Job Description: Artificial intelligence specialists usually work in the math and science departments of universities or in the research and development divisions of large corporations. AI specialists may design software, program expert systems, or develop robotic technologies.

Education: A master's or doctoral degree is required. Most artificial intelligence specialists have a degree in computer science or cognitive science.

Qualifications: Artificial intelligence specialists need to be trained in programming or systems analysis and be fluent in several computer languages. They must also be able to work well with others.

Salary: Between $75,000 and $100,000 per year

ConsScale, it measures the behavioral level of machine consciousness and compares it to living things. At the lowest level are life forms such as bacteria. The higher the level the machine reaches the more its behavior resembles the consciousness of humans.

To become self-aware, an intelligent system has to recognize key patterns in its own behavior. If an artificially intelligent machine can observe its own actions and the responses of others to those actions, then it recognizes the pattern of its *self*. It can create a self-model and so it is *self*-aware. Self-awareness can make it possible for a machine to deal with new problems that come up as it interacts with the environment and other individuals and enable it to recognize the possible result of its actions. For example, it will recognize that if it chooses to perform a particular action, then a particular result will occur. Once an intelligent machine reaches this point, it is ready to make decisions based on its own will rather than on the will of its programmer. It is ready to think freely.

Junichi Takeno, a professor at Meiji University in Japan, has been investigating self-awareness in robots using a test that requires use of a mirror. Many researchers use mirrors to test whether a living creature is self-aware. The researcher puts a mark, or a sticker, on the subject's face. If the subject sees the mark or sticker in the mirror and reaches up to touch the mark on his or her own face, the subject has demonstrated self-awareness. Human children can usually pass the test when they are about two years old. In Takeno's test the robot must be able to tell the difference between its own reflection in a mirror and that of another identical robot. In 2005 Takeno announced that he had developed a robot that was able to pass that test. How a self-aware form of strong AI will interact with humans is still unknown.

The Singularity

In 1993 math professor and science-fiction writer Vernor Vinge published a research paper titled *The Coming Technological Singularity: How to Survive in the Post-Human Era.*

Futurist Ray Kurzweil speaks at a conference in 2007. He has predicted the date for Singularity, the point at which artificial intelligence surpasses human intelligence, as 2045.

THE FUTURE OF AI?

In 2008 robotics expert Hans Moravec suggested that by the year 2050 robot intelligence would surpass that of humans – an event known as "the Singularity." At the time of Moravec's statement, many personal computers were already capable of 10,000 MIPS.

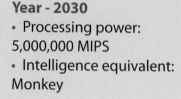

Year - 2020
- Processing power: 100,000 MIPS
- Intelligence equivalent: Mouse

Year - 2040
- Processing power: 100,000,000 MIPS
- Intelligence equivalent: Human

Year - 2010
- Processing power: 20,000 MIPS (millions of instructions per second)
- Intelligence equivalent: Lizard

Year - 2030
- Processing power: 5,000,000 MIPS
- Intelligence equivalent: Monkey

Source: Hans Moravec. "Rise of the Robots – The Future of Artificial Intelligence." *Scientific American*. March 23, 2009. www.scientificamerican.com/article.cfm?id=rise-of-the-robots.

In the paper he suggests that the time may come when AI surpasses human intelligence, an event he calls the singularity. "Within 30 years, we will have the technological means to create superhuman intelligence," Vinge writes. "Shortly after, the human era will be ended."[37]

Singularity University

Singularity University was founded in 2008 by Raymond Kurzweil and Peter H. Diamandis, chief executive of the X-Prize Foundation, an organization that gives cash awards to designers who break technological barriers. The mission of the university is to bring together and train experts involved in the development of technologies, such as biotechnology, nanotechnology, and artificial intelligence. It is located on the grounds of the NASA Ames Research Center in Moffett Field, California. Larry Page, a cofounder of the search engine Google, and some of Google's earliest employees helped establish Singularity University.

The school is not a traditional four-year university. It holds a ten-week summer graduate studies program for graduate and postgraduate students and ten-day executive programs for corporate executives and government leaders. The university also offers ten academic tracks related to advanced technology, including topics such as future studies, computing systems, human enhancement, robotics, and AI. One of the goals of the university is to bring together students and experts to consider ways to use advanced technologies, including artificial intelligence, to solve problems facing modern society.

Many people point out that AI agents will have access to the designs and programs used to create them. This opens the possibility of such machines redesigning and improving themselves. As they continue to upgrade, they may reach a level of superintelligence with abilities thousands of times greater than that of humans. At that point humans may be unable to keep up and the singularity line will be crossed. Author and inventor Raymond Kurzweil (1948–) believes that will happen in the near future. "I set the date for the Singularity, representing a profound and disruptive transformation in human capability, as 2045," he says. "The non-biological intelligence created in that year will be one billion times more powerful than all human intelligence today."[38]

Ethical Behavior in Machines

Could self-aware robots or supercomputers become hostile toward humans? If the goals of intelligent machines do not match the goals of humans, there could be conflict. Some experts warn that such a situation could be dangerous unless humans plan ahead to ensure their own safety. There is likely to be a great difference between the way that machines and humans think, although they may arrive at the same conclusions. Ryszard Michalski (1937–2007), one of the pioneers of machine learning, the ability of computers to improve their performance over time by making corrections based on previous results, suggested that machine minds might be so unlike human minds that they could be considered an alien intelligence. Computer scientist Stephen Omohundro (1949–) states that all advanced AI systems will, "unless explicitly counteracted, exhibit a number of basic drives that could, without precautions, cause the AI to act in

A person extends a finger toward a robot programmed to mimic human actions.

ways that range from the disobedient to the dangerously unethical."[39] In an article in a 2007 issue of *AI Magazine* authors Michael Anderson and Susan Leigh Anderson write,

> The newly emerging field of machine ethics is concerned with adding an ethical dimension to machines. Unlike computer ethics, which has traditionally focused on ethical issues surrounding humans' use of machines, machine ethics is concerned with ensuring that the behavior of machines toward human users, and perhaps other machines as well, is ethically acceptable.[40]

Some experts in the field of AI think that the danger to humans will not be from supermachines that are hostile to humans, but from machines that do not care about humans at all and are indifferent to what happens to them. For these experts, the goal is to insert "friendliness safeguards" into early programs, so that computers can be designed to be sympathetic toward humans. Nick Bostrom, a professor of philosophy at Oxford University in England, states, "Basically we should assume that a superintelligence would be able to achieve whatever goals it has. Therefore, it is extremely important that the goals we endow it with, and its entire motivation system, is 'human friendly.'"[41]

Rights and Responsibilities

The creation of intelligent machines will also require humans to consider how such artificial life forms should be treated. South Korea is recognized for its commitment to advanced technology and may be a model for other countries. In 2007 the nation created *The Robot Ethics Charter*, an ethical code designed to help protect humans from being harmed by robots and to prevent humans from harming intelligent machines. Important goals of the charter include preserving human control over robots, protecting information gathered by robots, and preventing the use of robots for illegal purposes. It also covers standards for manufacturers and rules for

Robots created by the German Research Center for Artificial Intelligence play soccer at an exhibition in 2010.

users. A five-member team worked together to draw up the list of guidelines. The government hopes that the plan will set ethical standards concerning the treatment and acceptable uses of robots. The Korean Ministry of Information and Communication notes that robots are expected to develop strong AI in the near future. A 2007 South Korean government report states, "Robots would routinely carry out surgery by the year 2018" and "every South Korean household will have a robot by between 2015 and 2020."[42]

The European Robotics Research Network (EURON), a community of more than 225 academic and industrial groups doing research in robotics, also established a set of guidelines on the use of robots. Guidelines are already in place for advanced disciplines, such as nuclear physics and bioengineering. In 2006 the United Kingdom published a government study noting the possibility that by 2050 robots might be advanced enough to demand the same rights as human beings. A draft of the EURON proposal states, "In the 21st Century humanity will coexist with the first alien intelligence we have ever come into contact with—robots. It will be an event rich in ethical, social and economic problems."[43]

Legal Issues

If humans and robots are to coexist, society will have to address the danger that improper use of AI might present. Industrial robots have already accidentally injured and caused the death of humans. A man was killed in 1979 when he was struck by a robotic arm at a factory in the United States. A Japanese factory employee was killed in 1981 when he was working with a robot that he believed to be shut off. The robot activated and pushed the worker into another machine. In 2006 the *Economist Technology Quarterly* warned, "With robots now poised to emerge from their industrial cages and to move into homes and workplaces, roboticists [people who design, construct, and operate robots] are concerned about the safety implications beyond the factory floor."[44]

Who should be held accountable when a robot harms a human? Is the owner, the designer, or the manufacturer responsible? It is likely that such cases would be decided in civil court. "When the first robot carpet-sweeper sucks up a baby, who will be to blame?"[45] asks John Hallam, a professor at the University of Southern Denmark. As the intelligence of robots increases, will the machines themselves be considered at fault in an accident? Is it possible for a robot to commit a crime? The answers may depend on whether or not the robot is intelligent enough or is programmed to understand the difference between right and wrong. As of the early twenty-first century, no legal body in the world suggests that a robot can be held legally responsible for its actions.

In 2003 attorney Martine Rothblatt filed a motion in a mock trial (a pretend or practice trial held for educational purposes) at the International Bar Association conference in San Francisco, California. Her goal was to prevent a corporation from disconnecting an intelligent computer known as BINA48. Rothblatt pointed out that without laws to protect BINA48 the designer of conscious software is free to delete his or her software. In the end, the presiding judge ruled against the extension of human rights, although the jury, made up of the audience of lawyers, disagreed. They voted to extend human rights to the computer.

We Are Watching

A security center collects and analyzes data recorded by surveillance cameras at a train station in Milan, Italy.

As people consider the rights of machines, they will also have to determine whether intelligent machines may interfere with human lifestyles. One common concern with the rise of AI is the loss of privacy as surveillance systems

become common in many public places. Author James Vlahos says, "In the era of computer-controlled surveillance, your every move could be captured by cameras, whether you're shopping in the grocery store or driving on the freeway. Proponents say it will keep us safe, but at what cost?"[46]

An ABC News/*Washington Post* poll in July 2007 found that 71 percent of Americans favor increased video surveillance. Such systems are designed to prevent crime and keep people safe, but most cameras are controlled by computers with advanced software that is capable of gathering a great deal of information. For example, the system at Liberty Island in New York, where the Statue of Liberty is located, is able to detect an abandoned bag or backpack. It can keep track of visitors and note a person who has stayed on the island after closing. It can even identify crowd behavior that indicates a fight. The Internet is another area where personal privacy may be compromised. The issues include the use of spyware and text strings, called cookies, that may be employed to track users' browsing or shopping habits.

Venturing into the Unknown

The history of science and technology shows that every breakthrough or invention has both benefits and risks. There is no doubt that the development of AI will continue to bring change in the form of neural interfaces, cybernetics, nanotechnology, robotics, and much more. It is likely that in the coming decades new technologies will be introduced that have not yet been imagined. Some technologies are already drawing protests. Some people object to using insects as living sensors, the possible use of robots as soldiers, or the cybernetic blending of human and machine. Some researchers are concerned that a superior AI could overpower human society. But as Eliezer Yudkowsky, AI researcher and advocate of Friendly AI, says, "Technology is heading here. It will predictably get to the point of making artificial intelligence. The mere fact that you cannot predict exactly when it will happen down to the day is no excuse for closing your eyes and refusing to think about it."[47] It is important to remember that the many advances on the horizon are neither all good nor all bad. Technology is neutral and is defined by its use. It will be up to humanity to determine how the coming wave of AI will be used.

NOTES

Chapter 1: The First Steps

1. Quoted in Martin Beech. "On Seeing D2." University of Regina. http://hyperion.cc.uregina.ca/%7Eastro/On%20Seeing%20D2.pdf.
2. Quoted in Jeremy M. Norman, ed. *From Gutenberg to the Internet: A Sourcebook on the History of Information Technology.* Novato, CA, 2005, p. 235.
3. Alan Turning. "Computing Machinery and Intelligence." *MIND, A Quarterly Review of Psychology and Philosophy* 59, no. 236, 1950, pp. 433–460.
4. Quoted in Arkadiusz Janicki. "Computer Chess." www.slideshare.net/aerjotl/computer-chess.
5. J. McCarthy, M. L. Minsky, N. Rochester, and C. E. Shannon. "A Proposal for the Dartmouth Summer Research Project on Artificial Intelligence." August 31, 1955. http://www-formal.stanford.edu/jmc/history/dartmouth/dartmouth.html.
6. John Searle. "Minds, Brains and Programs." *Behavioral and Brain Sciences.* 3, no. 3, 1980, p. 12.

7. Drew McDermott. "How Intelligent Is Deep Blue." *New York Times,* May 14, 1997.

Chapter 2: Creating an Intelligent Machine

8. Quoted in Larry Greenemeier. "Machine Self-Awareness." *Scientific American,* June 2010. www.scientificamerican.com/podcast/episode.cfm?id=the-big-dozen-12-events-that-will-c-10-06-02.
9. Quoted in Linda S. Gottfredson. "Foreword." Special Issue, *Intelligence* 24, no. 1, 1997, p. 13. www.udel.edu/educ/gottfredson/reprints/1997specialissue.pdf.
10. Quoted in ScienceDaily. "Brain System Behind General Intelligence Discovered." ScienceDaily, February 23, 2010. www.sciencedaily.com/releases/2010/02/100222161843.htm.
11. Quoted in Emily Sohn. "Tiny Insect Brains Solve Big Problems." DiscoveryNews, November 16, 2009. http://news.discovery.com/animals/tiny-insect-brains-intelligence.html.

12. Greg Fish. "Are Insects the First Step in Creating AI?" Weird Things. January 9, 2010. http://worldofweirdthings.com/2010/01/09/are-insects-the-first-step-in-creating-a-i/.

13. Quoted in Jonah Lehrer. "Out of the Blue." SeedMagazine.com, March 3, 2008. http://seedmagazine.com/content/article/out_of_the_blue.

14. Quoted in Lehrer. "Out of the Blue."

15. McCarthy, Minsky, Rochester, and Shannon. "A Proposal for the Dartmouth Summer Research Project on Artificial Intelligence."

16. Quoted in AI Topics Editorial Board. "Natural Language: Understanding and Generating Text and Speech." AI Topics, June 12, 2010. www.aaai.org/AITopics/pmwiki/pmwiki.php/AITopics/NaturalLanguage.

17. Quoted in Jack Copeland. "What Is Artificial Intelligence?" AlanTuring.net, May 2000. www.alanturing.net/turing_archive/pages/Reference%20Articles/what_is_AI/What%20is%20AI02.html.

18. Ben Goertzel. "Artificial General Intelligence: Now Is the Time." KurzweilAI.net, April 9, 2007. www.kurzweilai.net/articles/art0701.html?printable=1.

Chapter 3: Intelligent Robots

19. Quoted in CBC News. "What Is a Robot?" CBC News, July 16, 2007. www.cbc.ca/news/background/tech/robotics/definition.html.

20. Nicholas Roy. Interview with the author. January 2011.

21. Quoted in Gordy Slack. "DASH to the Next Gen of Robots: Small, Cheap, and Feral." ACM TechNews, February 10, 2010. http://technews.acm.org/archives.cfm?fo=2010-02-feb/feb-10-2010.html.

22. Quoted in Ashlee Vance. "Merely Human? That's So Yesterday." *New York Times*, June 11, 2010. www.nytimes.com/2010/06/13/business/13sing.html.

23. Robin Marantz Henig. "The Real Transformers." *New York Times*, July 29, 2007.

Chapter 4: The Future of Artificial Intelligence

24. Rosalind W. Picard. "Does HAL Cry Digital Tears? Emotions and Computers." In David G. Stork ed., *HAL's Legacy: 2001's Computer as Dream and Reality.* Cambridge, MA: MIT Press, 1996.

25. Quoted in Duncan Graham-Rowe. "An Emotional Cat Robot." *Technology Review.* July 26, 2007. www.technologyreview.com/computing/19102/.

26. Quoted in Graham-Rowe. "An Emotional Cat Robot." www.technologyreview.com/computing/19102/.

27. McCarthy, Minsky, Rochester, and Shannon. "A Proposal for the

Dartmouth Summer Research Project on Artificial Intelligence."

28. Quoted in John Makulowich. "The Future of Virtual Reality." *USA Today.* www.usatoday.com/tech/columnist/ccmak005.htm.

29. Quoted in Christopher Ryan. "Virtual Reality in Marketing." *Direct Marketing*, April 2001, p. 59.

30. Ramesh Jain. "Digital Experience." *Communications of the ACM.* March 2001, p. 38.

31. Jack Judy. "Hybrid Insect MEMS (HI-MEMS)." Microsystem Technology Office, March 5, 2010. www.darpa.mil/mto/programs/himems/index.html#content.

32. Quoted in Baiju Parthan. "Technology: The Cyborgs Are Coming." *Life Positive*, December 2000. www.lifepositive.com/mind/evolution/technology/cyborg.asp.

33. Quoted in Vance. "Merely Human? That's So Yesterday."

34. Quoted in Francis Fukuyama. "Transhumanism." *Foreign Policy* 144, pp. 42–43.

35. Quoted in Nicholas Wade. "Researchers Say They Created a 'Synthetic Cell.'" *New York Times*, May 20, 2010.

Chapter 5: The Ethics of Artificial Intelligence

36. Gordon E. Moore. "Cramming More Components Onto Integrated Circuits." *Electronics*, April 19, 1965, p. 4.

37. Quoted in Vance. "Merely Human? That's So Yesterday."

38. Raymond Kurzweil. Interview by Janet Maslin. "The Singularity Is Near—An Amazing Future." Singularity.com. www.singularity.com/themovie/future.php.

39. Quoted in Michael Anderson and Susan Leigh Anderson. "Machine Ethics: Creating an Ethical Intelligent Agent." *AI Magazine* 28, no. 4, Winter 2007. www.aaai.org/ojs/index.php/aimagazine/article/view/2065/2052.

40. Anderson and Anderson. "Machine Ethics: Creating an Ethical Intelligent Agent," p. 15.

41. Quoted in Dustin Ingram. "The Singularity: Friendliness Theory." dustingram.com, August 11, 2009. www.dustingram.com/wiki/The_Singularity:_Friendliness_Theory.

42. Quoted in BBC News. "Robotic Age Poses Ethical Dilemma." BBC News, March 7, 2007. http://news.bbc.co.uk/2/hi/technology/6425927.stm.

43. Quoted in BBC News. "Robotic Age Poses Ethical Dilemma."

44. *The Economist Technology Quarterly*, "Trust Me, I'm a Robot." June 8, 2006. www.economist.com/node/700182945.

45. Quoted in John Glick. "Trust Me I'm a Robot, AI in the News." *AI Magazine* 27, no. 3, 2006. www.aaai.org/ojs/index.php/aimagazine/article/viewFile/1902/1800.

46. James Vlahos. "Surveillance Society: New High-Tech Cameras Are Watching You." *Popular Mechanics*, January 2008. www.popularmechanics.com/technology/military/4236865.

47. Quoted in Marcus Wohlsen. "What Will Happen When Machines Outthink Us?" MSNBC.com, September 2007. www.msnbc.msn.com/id/20676037/ns/technology_and_science-innovation.

GLOSSARY

3-D: A system or effect that adds a three-dimensional appearance to visual images, as in films.

algorithm: A logical step-by-step procedure for solving a mathematical problem.

biofuel: A fuel made from biological material such as plants.

boolean logic: A branch of algebra in which all operations are either true or false and all relationships between the operations can be expressed with operators such as *and* and *or*.

digital: Data represented in the form of numerical digits.

feedback: Useful information returned as the result of output by a machine or system.

genome: The full complement of genetic information that an organism inherits from its parents.

global positioning system (GPS): A satellite-based navigation system.

gyroscope: A device with a rotating wheel inside a circular frame used to measure orientation in space.

heuristic: Relating to a method of teaching that uses trial and error.

hydraulic: Relating to a device in which pressure applied to a piston is transmitted by a fluid to a larger piston.

memory: The part of a computer in which data is stored.

processor: The central processing unit of a computer.

silicon: A nonmetallic chemical found naturally in sand and many minerals.

software: Computer programs and applications.

vacuum tube: A device used to amplify, switch, otherwise modify, or create an electrical signal.

virtual: Existing in effect but not in fact or reality.

FOR MORE INFORMATION

Books

Roger Bridgman. *Robot*. New York: DK Eyewitness Books, 2004. A very visual book for young readers with plenty of interesting photos and sidebars.

Holly Cefrey. *Virtual Reality: Life in the Future*. Chicago, IL: Children's Press, 2002. An exploration of the technology involved in virtual reality and a look at its future in entertainment, education, science, and medicine.

Sylvia Engdahl. *Contemporary Issues Companion: Artificial Intelligence*. Farmington Hills, MI: Greenhaven Press, 2007. A collection of essays by different writers on topics such as robots and superintelligence.

Sandy Fritz. *Robotics and Artificial Intelligence: Hot Science*. North Mankato, MN: Smart Apple Media, 2003. An introduction to the field of robotics illustrated with plenty of color photographs.

Clive Gifford. *Robots*. New York: Atheneum, 2008. A complete guide to the modern world of robotics and a look ahead to the possibilities for the future.

Robert Greenberger. *Careers in Artificial Intelligence: Cutting-Edge Careers*. New York: Rosen, 2007. An overview of some of the great careers in artificial intelligence in fields such as robotics, health, space science, and game design.

Alex Woolf. *Artificial Intelligence: 21st Century Debates*. London: Hodder Wayland, 2002. A clearly written book on the origins and applications of AI. It includes fact boxes, debate suggestions, and viewpoints sections that reject and favor AI.

Websites

AI Topics (www.aaai.org). A large site with pages on every type of AI and a very helpful page for kids on how to write a school report on AI.

Computer History Museum (www.computerhistory.org). An overview of the museum exhibits, plenty of photos, and a great feature called "This Day in History."

Kismet (www.ai.mit.edu/projects/humanoid-robotics-group/kismet/). A website about Kismet the robot with research information and photos.

Robot Hall of Fame (www.robothall offame.org/unimate.html). A fun site that gives overviews of famous robots in science and science fiction.

SPARK (http://spark.irobot.com/cool_ stuff). Includes a robot photo gallery, interactive games, crafts, videos and a time line of robots.

INDEX

PICTURE CREDITS

Cover: Alperium/Shutterstock.com

animate4.com ltd./Photo Researchers, Inc., 76

AP Images/Douglas C. Pizac, 61

AP Images/George Widman, 26

AP Images/Koji Sasahara, 54

AP Images/Lisa Poole, 67

AP Images/NASA, 59

AP Images/Paul Sakuma, 86

© Bettman/Corbis, 50

© bilwissedition Ltd. & Co. KG/Alamy, 11

Bloomberg/Getty Images, 89

Bloomberg via Getty Images, 9

Christian Darkin/Photo Researchers, Inc., 80

David Kampfner/Getty Images News/ Getty Images, 78

Gale, Cengage Learning, 21, 35, 62, 70, 90

Hank Morgan/Photo Researchers, Inc., 72

Hulton Archive/Archive Photos/Getty Images, 24

© INTERFOTO/Alamy, 46

Jason Kempin/WireImage/Getty Images, 52

© Jim West/Alamy, 42

L. Birmingham/Custom Medical Stock, Inc., 38

© Mark Harmel/Alamy, 39

Matthew Naythons/Time & Life Images/ Getty Images, 8

Mauro Fermariello/Photo Researchers, Inc., 74

© Medical Health Care/Alamy, 63

Nigel Cattlin/Photo Researchers, Inc., 36

© Photos 12/Alamy, 12, 85

Pasquale Sorrentino/Photo Researchers, Inc., 92

Ralph Crane/Time & Life Pictures/ Getty Images, 9

Science & Society Picture Library/Getty Images, 15, 16, 17, 19

Sean Gallup/Getty Images News/Getty Images, 94

SSPL via Getty Images, 8

Vittorio Zunino Celotto/Getty Images News/Getty Images, 96

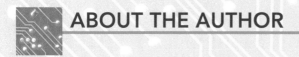

ABOUT THE AUTHOR

Q. L. Pearce has written more than one hundred books for children and more than thirty classroom workbooks and teacher manuals on the topics of reading, science, math, and values. Pearce has written science-related articles for magazines; regularly gives presentations at schools, bookstores, and libraries; and is a frequent contributor to the educational program of the Los Angeles County Fair. She is an assistant regional adviser for the Society of Children's Book Writers and Illustrators.